THREE YEARS AMONG THE COMANCHES
THE NARRATIVE OF NELSON LEE, THE TEXAS
RANGER

Nelson Lee

Table of Contents

CHAPTER 1

The course of my life, which has now passed the boundary of half a century, has varied so far from the ordinary current of human existence that many of my friends, on whose judgment I rely, have urged me to furnish a statement of my history for publication. I have yielded to their solicitations, and shall endeavor, in the progress of this narrative, to describe the adventures it has been my fortune to encounter, especially while a volunteer among the Texas Rangers, and afterwards a captive among the Comanche Indians, without color or exaggeration.

I was born at Brownsville, near Watertown, Jefferson County, New York, in 1807. Parmer Lee, my father, was a farmer at that place, having always been engaged in agricultural pursuits, except a short period during the last war, when he joined the forces under Brown raised for the defense of the frontier. Our family was originally from Catskill on the Hudson, the native town of my grandfather, one of the soldiers of the Revolution, who participated in the battles of Saratoga and was present at the surrender of Burgoyne.

During my minority I was remarkable for nothing I can now recall, save a most hardy constitution and athletic frame, and an intense longing to rove out into the world. In early youth I had resolved, as soon as released from paternal restraint, to pass the horizon that bounded my quiet home, and learn as far as in my power of all the lands that lay beyond. Indulging this propensity, my first adventure from home, on coming to man's estate, was a trip upon a raft from Sackets Harbor on Lake Ontario, through the St. Lawrence to Quebec. In the character of boatman and raftsman I remained on this river more or less for several years, sometimes sailing among the Thousand Islands, at others descending the swift rapids, but nothing occurring in the meantime of sufficient interest to relate.

In 1831 the attention of the whole country was turned towards the Black Hawk War. The obstinate resistance of that celebrated chief who was desolating the homes of the settlers in the Far West rendered it necessary for government to resort to severe measures in order to subdue him. In answer to a call for volunteers I joined Captain Hall, in May of that year, at Buffalo. We left the latter place in the steamer Eagle, directing our course up the lake for the harbor of Detroit. The cholera, however, breaking out upon the voyage, which resulted in the death of several on board, we were not permitted to approach Detroit, but forced to land at a point known, I believe, as Gratiot. Here we met General Scott, who gave orders, in consequence of the great violence of the epidemic, that the forces should proceed westward in small detached parties. Accordingly, a company of four of us found our way across the country as far as Prairie du Chien, where we were disappointed to learn that the hitherto indomitable Black Hawk with his Prophet and chief warriors had been taken captive, and that the war was closed.

Not desiring to turn back, but, on the contrary, anxious to visit other localities of which I had heard much, I journeyed onward to St. Louis, and after a brief delay, proceeded to New Orleans, visiting every town of importance on both sides the Father of Rivers, between those cities. Lingering but a short time in New Orleans, I set forward once more, and making the best progress I was able, eventually reached Washington, where, receiving the appointment of master's mate, I was sent on board the ship Delaware, then lying at Portsmouth, near Norfolk, and sailed for New York. Here, I was transferred to the Ontario, sloop of war, Captain Salters, and turning my course south again, departed for the distant region of Brazil. Arriving at Rio Janeiro, after enduring much suffering from the want of fresh water, we were ordered by the American consul to sail in pursuit of pirates which at that time were known to be lurking in the vicinity of the island of St. Thomas and along the African coast. Our search, however, was unsuccessful, though we pursued it to the island to open the doors of his prison cells, thinking we might perhaps, find the objects of our pursuit among the malefactors they contained.

Returned to Rio Janeiro from this fruitless cruise, memorable only for the smallpox which decimated our crew, we joined the main squadron then lying at this port, Commodore Renshaw commanding. From thence we frequently sailed on voyages more or less remote—sometimes ascending the Rio Plato, blockaded by the Portuguese—sometimes protecting consuls in the seaport towns of South America—from time to time transferred from one vessel to another, until at last in the year 1838, after seven years of wandering, I found myself on board the sloop of war Fairfield, anchored off the metropolis of my native state, having traversed a large portion of the western continent, and experienced much of good and evil fortune, both on land and sea.

Shortly after, I was transferred to the sloop of war Preble, Captain Breese, which had been ordered to proceed to Newfoundland to cruise among the fishermen. For some alleged encroachment, two American fishing smacks had been seized by an English man-of-war, an act regarded by our government as a violation of its rights, and Captain Breese was ordered to release them. He entered the harbor of Prince Edward's Island, and anchoring within short gunshot of the offending man-of-war, haughtily demanded the deliverance of the captured vessels, giving him but twenty-five minutes to comply. It was a moment of extreme anxiety, and I confess myself relieved of an oppressive burden on unexpectedly hearing the demand acceded to. We escorted the fishermen out into the open sea and separated, they steering for Portsmouth in New Hampshire, we returning by the way of Halifax to Boston, where I quitted finally the naval service of the United States.

Wandering around Boston some weeks, entirely unoccupied, time began to drag wearily away. To me, a life of inactivity was irksome, and casting about for some sort of employment congenial to my tastes, the rumors of troublous times in Texas at length arrested my attention. I had but a vague knowledge of events transpiring there; sufficient, however, to create within me a desire to turn my steps thitherward; and accordingly, I seized the first opportunity which offered of departing in that direction, by taking passage on the barque 'Gentleman' bound for New Orleans.

We had a smooth sea and favorable winds until opposite a point, known as "the hole in the wall," near the coast of Florida, where we were overtaken by a storm, more violent than any I had ever previously experienced in all my seafaring life. Mistaking a light on our starboard for Key West, the captain, in the confusion of the storm, ran directly on a reef. In this situation we all instinctively understood that rescue was beyond hope. Without any definite motive I clambered into the rigging, and there clung during the long hours of a night of terror, such as is not often allotted unto suffering man to bear. Swinging to and fro in the utter darkness, expecting momentarily to be swallowed up by the remorseless waves that roared and dashed beneath, the minutest memories of the past came back upon me with a power beyond description. I was reconciled, at length, to the idea of death, but it was a grief I could not overcome, to think I should pass away forever, and none of all my kindred ever know my fate. I could have willingly released my grasp, and sunk into the sea with a sense of rest, could some electric power have been given me, to convey to my distant relatives and friends a knowledge of my unhappy lot, and how and where I died.

My contemplations, as may well be imagined, were gloomy and sorrowful indeed; nevertheless, "I still lived." Hour after hour passed drearily away; but at last the sun, which seemed to have lingered ages on its eternal round, rose above the horizon in the east. Gradually the winds died away as the light overspread the wide expanse, and the furies which had shrieked around us through the night disappeared, as if ashamed to continue their revels in the face of day. Better still, we presently discovered boats approaching us from the shore, the dim outline of which was barely visible to the eye. They proved to be wreckers, who gain a precarious livelihood in their business, along that dangerous coast, and fortunately, as unexpectedly, succeeded in bringing us safe to land. I mention this incident with some degree of feeling, because, though I have passed through many perils since, as the reader will hereafter see, this impressed me so powerfully that time can never wear away the dread which it inspired.

We were conducted to Apalachicola, from whence, in due time, I proceeded to Galveston, and there, at once, joined the Texas navy about to send a force to the coast of Yucatan. The object of this expedition was to draw the Mexicans away from Texas. The little squadron I accompanied was commanded by Commodore Moore. We had an engagement off Yucatan, which, though severe, resulted in victory to neither party, and after a few months' cruising returned to Galveston. There I determined to abandon the sea forever, and going back into the interior, traversed the wide prairies that stretch away toward the borders of Mexico, and halting at Seguin, a point on the Guadaloupe, soon entered on the stirring life of a Texas Ranger.

In the foregoing chapter I have compressed into as brief a space as possible the events of my history from the time I left my father's house up to 1840. They are commonplace, but the career upon which I then entered, as I said in the beginning, runs not in the ordinary current of existence. It has been indeed "stranger than fiction," and as I look back upon it from the quiet I now enjoy, seems more like a feverish dream than a strange reality.

CHAPTER 2

At the time of my arrival in Texas, the country was in an unsettled state. For a long period of time a system of border warfare had existed between the citizens of Texas and Mexico, growing out of the declaration of independence on the part of the young republic. Marauding parties from beyond the Rio Grande kept the settlers of western Texas in a state of constant agitation and excitement. Besides these annoyances, the inhabitants of other sections were perpetually on the alert to defend themselves against those savage tribes which roamed over the vast region to the north, and which, not infrequently, stole down among the settlers, carrying away their property and putting them to death.

This condition of affairs necessarily resulted in bringing into existence the Texas Rangers, a military order as peculiar as it has become famous. The extensive frontier exposed to hostile inroads, together with the extremely sparse population of the country, rendered any other force of comparatively small avail. The qualifications necessary in a genuine Ranger were not, in many respects, such as are required in the ordinary soldier. Discipline, in the common acceptation of the term, was not regarded as absolutely essential. A fleet horse, an eye that could detect the trail, a power of endurance that defied fatigue, and the faculty of "looking through the double sights of his rifle with a steady arm,"—these distinguished the Ranger, rather than any special knowledge of tactics. He was subjected to no "regulation uniform," though his usual habiliments were buckskin moccasins and overhauls, a roundabout and red shirt, a cap manufactured by his own hands from the skin of the coon or wildcat, two or three revolvers and a bowie knife in his belt, and a short rifle on his arm. In this guise, and well mounted, should he measure eighty miles between the rising and setting sun, and then, gathering his blanket around him, lie down to rest upon the prairie grass with his saddle for a pillow, it would not, at all, occur to him he had performed an extraordinary day's labor.

The compensation received from government at that time was one dollar a day, and finding no other employment which seemed to me more remunerative or attractive, I joined Captain Cameron at San Patricio, then ranging in the vicinity of the Rio Grande. He was a Scotchman—a noble and brave man—who in very early life had left his native heather, and in the course of time established himself on the banks of the Nueces. During the disturbances which distracted the country, his intelligence, chivalry, and force of character naturally drew towards him the attention of his fellow citizens, as one upon whom they might lean for protection. His company consisted of forty-five men. My first experience in Indian warfare was an engagement with a roving band of Comanches, whom we suddenly encountered near Casa Blanca, during one of our excursions beyond the Nueces. They were put to flight after a sharp interchange of bullets on one side and arrows on the other; not, however, until I had become most emphatically impressed with a due sense of their brave and warlike character. They are a numerous and powerful tribe whose range extends from the headwaters of the Guadaloupe to the base of the Rocky Mountains, and of whose habits, dispositions, and mode of life I shall have much to say before this narrative concludes.

A short time subsequent to this adventure we obtained information that a considerable body of Mexicans had crossed the border and were somewhere in our vicinity. While on the lookout for them, we met, one day, the forces under General Davis, at Panta Clan. His company, having listened to extravagant rumors relative to the great number of Mexicans on the march, some of them rating it as high as three thousand well-armed and effective men, had become alarmed. During the night the most of them flocked to our encampment near by, discussing the all-absorbing question of the probable whereabouts of the enemy. At this very time, while we were indulging in all manner of surmises, the wily Mexicans had crept into their camp, and seizing every description of property on which they could lay their hands, retired without loss or molestation. The next morning, however, they presented themselves and offered battle, and though far outnumbering our united forces, we compelled them to retreat after a contest of two hours, taking from them, in addition to the spoils of the previous night, more than forty mules.

Though little was said about it at the time, a story eventually spread abroad that General Davis did not bear himself with becoming bravery on this occasion. It was alleged he abandoned his quarters, permitting the Indians to plunder them without resistance, through cowardice. Years after, while a candidate for office of delegate to the convention from his district on the Trinity, his political opponents endeavored to compass his defeat by representing him a poltroon at the battle of Panta Clan. Happening to be present at a barbecue where the subject was discussed, I was called upon to give my version of the affair, and in a political speech, the first and last I have ever made, fully exonerated him from the charge. My testimony seemed to be satisfactory, and the general was elected. He is now one of the largest landholders and most respected and prominent citizens of Texas.

It was not long after the Panta Clan engagement, while we were in the vicinity of Seguin, that Ben McCullough, with sixteen others including myself, were detached from the main body and sent out as spies. McCullough was a brave fellow, a tall, straight man, over six feet high, raw-boned, light, sandy hair, extremely reserved in manner, with keen black eyes which shone like diamonds. We presently struck a wide trail leading to the south, and following it, soon came in sight of some seven hundred Comanches, near the Lavaca River. Unable to cope with so formidable a body, we hovered in their vicinity, keeping them constantly under observation. They continued their march in the direction of the coast until they reached, at length, the settlement of Lindville, on Matagorda Bay, which they attacked and burned, killing four men, and carrying away three women as prisoners. From a distant height we witnessed this affair, entirely unable to render any effectual resistance. Runners, however, were dispatched in hot haste to General Burleson on the Colorado, conveying information of what had transpired, and requesting reinforcements.

True to his chivalrous nature, Burleson, who never waited a second call when danger was to be met or a duty was to be performed, sent forward as many as he could; so that, by the time we had tracked the marauders on their retreat as far as Plum Creek, our numbers had increased to three hundred. There we resolved to attack them.

In concluding upon the plan of attack, our great object was to rescue the captured women. It was ascertained, as we anticipated, that they were with the old warriors in the rear of their encampment. A portion of our force, accordingly, made a wide circuit, and falling stealthily upon that point succeeded in saving harmless two of the captives, the other being stabbed to death by an Indian before making his escape.

As I approached with another detachment of my comrades from a different direction, a buckshot struck me near the elbow, passing up the arm to the shoulder blade, where it yet remains. It was my bridle arm, causing me to drop the rein, and in consequence, my horse unexpectedly bore me directly into their midst. Perceiving my perilous situation, the

Rangers rushed after me without awaiting the word of command. A scene of terrible confusion followed, which terminated finally in a complete victory in our favor and the recovery of all the property stolen at the sack of Lindville.

My six months' term of service under Cameron now expired, and bidding him adieu, I journeyed to San Antonio, and from thence to Seguin on the Guadaloupe, where I had taken up my residence. Afterwards I marched with Cameron to Mier, but not under his command. He was, indeed, a remarkable personage, as true a friend of Texas as any who have ever fought her battles or yielded up their lives in her defense, and I cannot forbear alluding briefly, in this connection, to his subsequent career and melancholy fate.

In the famous attack on Mier, in 1842, he was taken prisoner, and was one of those unfortunate men who, in violation of solemn articles of capitulation, were marched in irons on that long and weary journey towards the dungeons of Mexico, the account of which constitutes one of the saddest chapters in all history. After surviving the desperate attack upon the guards at Salado, and drawing a "white bean" at the bloody decimation of the captives on their rearrest, the Dictator of Mexico could not rest content while one who had proved himself such an indomitable foe was permitted to exist. Green, in his history of the expedition against Mier gives the following description of the closing scene of his life:

"About eight o'clock at night," he says, "a menial murderer, with a pair of epaulets upon his shoulders, and a guard of mounted men under broad-brimmed hats, arrived with orders from the tyrant Santa Anna, to shoot the bold and beloved Captain Ewin Cameron. He was unchained from his partner, Colonel William F. Wilson, and with his interpreter, Alfred Thurmond, taken out of prison and kept under a separate guard until morning, when he was conducted to the rear of the village, the place of execution. A priest, the usual attendant of Mexican executions, was in waiting, and when asked if he wished to confess to the Holy Father, promptly answered, 'No! throughout life I believe I have lived an upright man, and if I have to confess, it shall be to my Maker.' His arms were then tied with a cord at the elbows and drawn back, and when the guard advanced to bandage his eyes, he said to his interpreter, 'Tell them no! Ewin Cameron can now, as he has often done before for the liberty of Texas, look death in the face without winking.' So saying, he threw his hat and blanket on the ground, opened the bosom of his hunting shirt, presented his naked breast, and gave the word 'Fire!' when his noble soul passed into another and we trust a better world."

He was about thirty-six years of age at the time he was murdered—as we have already said, a native of Scotland, tall and well proportioned, weighing nearly two hundred pounds, and of extraordinary physical power, which was in perfect keeping with his manly countenance and courageous heart. Thus died Ewen Cameron, the Ranger of the Rio Grande, and long, very long, will the patriotic citizens of his adopted state cherish him in their memories, as one whose bosom was bared to every danger in their defense, and whose life, at last, was sacrificed to the cause of liberty.

CHAPTER 3

Returned to Seguin, at the conclusion of my first campaign, the business I adopted for a livelihood, then a common one in that region, was capturing wild horses, and after breaking them to the saddle or harness, disposing of them to the planters. Sometimes I purchased from the Mexicans those which had already been subdued, and collecting a drove, would set out on a sort of horse-peddling speculation. Frequently these excursions extended into Louisiana, where profitable customers were generally to be found among the cotton and sugar growers on the bayous. They usually cost me, when purchased, four or five dollars a head, and were sold for a price ranging from fifteen to thirty, so that with industry and good luck, it was capable of being made a remunerative and, as it was to me, a congenial occupation.

At length, however, the country again rang with a call for volunteers, though previous to this time, I have omitted to relate, the men of the famous Santa Fe Expedition had departed on their disastrous journey. I had arranged with Ben McCullough and others to make one of this party; in fact accompanied it a long distance above Austin, but there becoming prostrated by a violent attack of chills and fever, which rendered a further advance painful to myself and inconvenient to the party, I was induced most reluctantly to turn back. Retracing my steps to Austin, I lingered idly in the neighborhood of the Colorado until health returned, when, responding to the call to arms, I entered on my second campaign as a Texas Ranger, by joining Jack Hays at San Antonio.

There are few readers in this country, I venture to conjecture, whose ears have not become familiar with the name of Jack Hays. It is inseparably connected with the struggle of Texas for independence, and will live in the remembrance of mankind so long as the history of that struggle shall survive. In the imagination of most persons he undoubtedly figures as a rough, bold giant, bewhiskered like a brigand, and wielding the strength of Hercules. On the contrary, at the period of which I write, he was a slim, slight, smooth-faced boy, not over twenty years of age, and looking younger than he was in fact. In his manners he was unassuming in the extreme, a stripling of few words, whose quiet demeanor stretched quite to the verge of modesty. Nevertheless, it was this youngster whom the tall, huge-framed brawny-armed campaigners hailed unanimously as their chief and leader when they had assembled together in their uncouth garb on the grand plaza of Bexar. It was a compliment as well deserved as it was unselfishly bestowed, for young as he was, he had already exhibited abundant evidence that, though a lamb in peace, he was a lion in war; and few, indeed, were the settlers, from the coast to the mountains of the north, or from the Sabine to the Rio Grande, who had not listened in wonder to his daring, and gloried in his exploits.

On a previous page I have given the general appearance of a Ranger, and have now nothing further in particular to add in that regard. Perhaps I should have said that if he was more sensitive in one point than in another, it was in regard to the condition and qualities of his horse. So well was this feeling understood, and the necessity which created it appreciated, that every animal remarkable for its power and speed was secured by the inhabitants, far and wide, for the service of the Rangers. It may, therefore, be supposed that they were well provided for in this respect. The horse I rode was a gallant black, clean-limbed, fleet as the wind, and recognized the name of Prince. He was a native of New York, and had been sent to Galveston when a two-year-old, as a present to Colonel Walton, the mayor of the city. He had more than once almost taken the life of the Colonel's son, and was of such a savage and vicious temper that he determined to get rid of him. He happened to fall into my possession, and for years we lived together, mutually sharing in numerous adventures, in the hunt and on the trail, in peace and war, the most intimate of companions. In the course of his experience he came to regard a Mexican or Indian with intense hatred, and in the confusion and shock of battle, with his teeth and heels often rendered as effectual service as the armed rider on his back.

There was something less than fifty of us, marshaled under Hays in the square of San Antonio, prepared to obey the order of President Houston, to scour the frontier in search of marauding bands of Mexicans and Indians. Our provisions consisted of a homoeopathic quantity of corn meal, coffee, sugar, and salt, in addition to which the citizens came out and filled the gourds which hung from our Spanish saddles with whisky, when, reining into line, we waved our coonskin caps to the populace, and galloped from the city.

Our destination was the headwaters of the Sevilla. Some three or four days subsequent to our departure, while dismounted on the banks of a small stream, one of the men who had gone out to bring in a deer for dinner, came flying back with the intelligence that Mexicans were approaching. In an instant we were in our saddles, and hurrying forward, presently discovered a company of some eighty Mexicans, with a large number of unmounted horses. They shifted their course as soon as we hove in sight, whereupon Hays dashed forward on a keen run, and riding up close to them, in a loud voice ordered a halt. The order was disregarded, when, spurring our horses to their utmost speed, we rounded a point of timber, presenting ourselves directly in their front. Of necessity, a fight ensued. In less time than I have been describing our maneuvers, the two parties were intermingled, interchanging thrusts and blows in a hand-to-hand encounter. It was a terrific onslaught, but of short duration. How it happened under the circumstances has ever been to me a matter of wonder; nevertheless, it is a fact, that only one of our men was slightly wounded, while half of their number, over forty, were killed outright, ten wounded, and the remainder taken prisoners. We conducted them back to San Antonio, entering the city amidst the most extravagant demonstrations of delight and triumph. The leaders were handed over to the civil authorities, by whom they were tried, convicted and hung, it appearing on investigation they were simply robbers returning from the pillage of LaGrange, on the Colorado. In the history of Texas this affair is mentioned as the battle of Sevilla, but amongst those engaged in it, it is always alluded to as the "Sevilla Scrape."

But a short time elapsed when rumors filled the town that Indians were ravaging the settlements along the Guadaloupe. Now, for the first time, we had furnished ourselves with Colt's revolvers, instruments of death, destined thereafter to figure prominently in the wild warfare of Texas. We sallied forth once more, without any definite object in view, save watching closely for trails, as we rode leisurely along. Our only amusement was hunting deer, with which the prairies abounded; a pastime we indulged in as much for the excitement it afforded as the venison steaks it furnished us in the camp.

At length, little apprehending danger, we halted at a locality known in that region as "The Forks." It is a sharp point of land at the intersection of Walker's Creek and the Guadaloupe. On three sides it is surrounded by a high, rocky, perpendicular bluff, from fifty to a hundred feet in height, and not far back from the extreme point, where we were encamped, as it were, at the base of the triangle, rose a high hill. Early in the morning, one of the party, while at breakfast, discovered an Indian horseman on the height, evidently a spy. Presently another made his appearance by his side. For some time we watched these apparitions as they appeared and vanished, until we became fully satisfied they were the outrunners of a numerous party, and that we were completely hemmed in. Experience taught us, at once, that the main body was collected on the opposite slope of the hill, and that our position was critical in the extreme. In this emergency, Hays called us together, as was his custom always under circumstances of peculiar peril, and addressed us. After setting forth the imminent dangers that evidently surrounded us, he stated the course he had resolved to adopt, if it met our approbation, which it did, unanimously. Mounting at once, we rode directly towards the horsemen on the height, at a slow pace, waving branches, and making every conceivable sign of peace. Halfway up the ascent, the Indian group on the summit, which till now had gazed motionlessly down upon us, their outline standing out clear and distinct between us and the sky beyond, suddenly wheeled and disappeared. That instant Jack Hays turned to the right, and calling on us in a low but determined voice to follow, we swept, like a tornado, round the side of the mountain, taking the Indians completely by surprise. They were two hundred in number, and fought well and bravely, but our revolvers, fatal as they were astonishing, put them speedily to flight.

In this encounter with the Comanches, memorable thereafter as the battle of Walker's Creek, with the loss of only three men and four wounded, we left ninety of our enemies dead upon the field. Long after, while again ranging in that quarter, I beheld their bones bleaching in the sun.

Connected with this battle of Walker's Creek there were many incidents of an interesting and thrilling character. Among our number was one known as Big Sam Taylor. At the first onset, an arrow struck him near the eye, passing downwards through his cheek, and out by the side of his neck. In attempting to extract it, the upper portion broke off, leaving the remainder in the wound. Nevertheless, in this condition he fought through the entire engagement, afterwards recovering, though henceforward bearing a most ugly scar.

Near the close of the fight, Hays came upon a chief lying on the ground, with a broken thigh. He attempted to take him prisoner, but the prostrate warrior had plainly resolved to yield his liberty only with his life. Quick as a flash of light, he fixed an arrow to his bow, sending it to the heart of a Ranger named Mott, one of the three we unfortunately lost. He struggled against his conquerors with all the strength and fierceness his broken limb permitted him to exercise, nor would he, in the least, yield the measure of a hair, until a pistol ball had sent the stern old warrior to his eternal rest.

CHAPTER 4

It was an invariable custom while ranging on the frontier, especially when there was any probability an enemy was in the neighborhood, to pursue the following mode of life: Two hours, more or less, before sunset, we halted; always by a stream of water if possible. Some gathered wood and kindled a fire—some took charge of the horses, while others sallied out in quest of game for supper. Having satisfied the cravings of appetite, as soon as darkness began to overspread the prairie, we mounted, and riding an hour or more directly out of our general course, halted for the night in the most secluded situation we could discover. The object was to sleep as far as possible from the smoke, which the cooking of our supper necessarily created, and which, as it curled into the air, was impossible to hide from the observation of the enemy. Two hours before daybreak we were again on our horses, and thus we passed day after day, and night after night, scouring in all directions the wide plains of Texas.

A day or two subsequent to the battle of Walker's Creek, while on our way back towards San Antonio, we reined up, as usual, to prepare our evening repast near the bank of a small stream. It happened that I dismounted by a cluster of musquete bushes, and as I struck the ground an enormous rattlesnake bit me on the ankle. I had before frequently witnessed the deadly effects resulting from the bite of these venomous reptiles, and I confess, my nerves, which had not failed me in the hour of battle and in the face of death, were now completely unstrung. A sickening, dreadful sensation came over me, terrible beyond all force of language to convey—a sense of sorrow that I had not fallen in the recent battle and escaped the horror of going to my long account in such an abominable way.

There was a Spaniard among our number who witnessed the incident. He immediately thrust his knife through the serpent's neck, pinning it to the ground, and instantly began cutting portions of flesh from the still living and wriggling monster, and applying it to the wound. I could feel it draw, and in a few minutes the white poultice thus applied would change to a perfect green. These applications were continued until nearly the entire body of the snake was used. The remedy proved effectual, inasmuch as I suffered nothing from it afterwards save a slight soreness, though from that time forward, I always experienced an instinctive dread on approaching a musquete thicket, far more disagreeable than when charging an enemy.

I once met with a somewhat similar adventure on the Aransas, near the Gulf. Stopping a few days at the ranche of an old acquaintance, to while away an idle hour, I started out on a deer hunt with one of his Mexican herdsmen. It happened that my first shot broke both the hind legs of a noble stag, when he plunged into the stream, at this point some fifty yards in width, swimming to the opposite shore, but unable to ascend the bank. Anxious to secure him I swam across, having only a belt around me, which held a hunting knife. As I approached, he made for the other shore, when he was again wounded by the Mexican. Several times both of us crossed the stream. On my last passage, when perhaps two-thirds over, I discovered at no great distance, a huge alligator making directly towards me. He was at least fourteen feet in length, and had been undoubtedly attracted by the blood which tainted the water. My first impulse was to draw my knife and turn upon him, but a second thought determined me to exercise that discretion which is the better part of valor, and accordingly, I venture the assertion that in all aquatic feats of which we have any account, there never has been known a specimen of "taller swimming" than I then and there performed. Fortunately, I reached the shore and succeeded in scrambling to the top of the bank just as the monster came like a great battering ram against it. It was a luxury to plant a rifle ball in that alligator's eye, and as he rolled over, a lifeless heap, to indulge the satisfaction of knowing that he would frighten the wits out of a poor devil no more forever.

Others have often expressed their entire indifference to these reptiles, and really seemed to disregard them altogether, but for my own part, the alligator, the centipede, the rattlesnake, and, more than all, the cottonmouth moccasin, during my excursions over the prairies and along the rivers of Mexico and Texas, were sources of perpetual apprehension and annoyance.

We arrived in San Antonio, after the battle of Walker's Creek, sooner than we were expected, and surprised a robbing party, Mexican guerrillas, in possession of the city; the inhabitants entirely at their mercy. The American residents kept themselves secluded, the stores were closed, and the ordinary business of the town had utterly subsided. They were insolent and lawless beyond endurance, and carried on their depredations to an extent almost incredible. They were a portion of a band of five or six hundred desperadoes, commanded by one Antonio Perez, a native of

Bexar, and well known to all its citizens. He had formerly rendered effective service in the cause of Texas, was a man of property and favorably esteemed, but like many of his countrymen, eventually proved a traitor to the friends of liberty, descending from the position of a patriot to the level of a thief and robber.

Receiving intelligence of the situation of affairs, we crept cautiously into the town late at night, and joined by the citizens, succeeded in surrounding the house where the greater portion of them were assembled at a grand fandango, before they were aware. Suddenly entering the house, a furious and indiscriminate attack began, in which we killed sixteen and took eight prisoners, repaying their swaggering and lawless insolence with compound usury. The prisoners were delivered over to the judicial authorities, two of whom were tried, found guilty and shot.

A few weeks after this event orders arrived from President Houston, directing us to set out again on a reconnoitering excursion along the border of Mexico. The object of the expedition was to ascertain whether it was true, as everywhere reported, that a large Mexican force was concentrating somewhere beyond the river, preparatory to another warlike descent upon the country.

No time was lost in getting ready to carry the President's orders into execution, and soon, following the lead of Jack Hays, we had left behind us all that wide extent of country stretching from San Antonio to the Rio Grande, which latter we crossed at a point ten miles below Laredo. We were now upon Mexican territory and were impressed with the necessity of advancing with great caution, well aware the fate of spies awaited us should we happen to be surrounded and overwhelmed. Our progress was necessarily slow; nevertheless, we continued on our course down the west shore, passing numerous villages and haciendas, yet entirely eluding recognition.

The popular opinion has sometimes prevailed that the Rio Grande is full of shoals and rocks, subject to become almost dry in the autumnal season. So far from this being correct, it is always navigable, at the lowest stage of water, any portion of the year, from far above Laredo. It is, indeed, a beautiful river, averaging four hundred yards in width, with high bluffs generally on one shore or the other, and the opposite side always a fertile bottom. This river resembles the Ohio more than any I recollect to have seen, and is far superior for steamboat navigation to any other upon the Gulf of Mexico, west of the Mississippi. The alluvion is almost exclusively on the west bank, and is capable of being brought into the highest state of cultivation, while the eastern shore is lined with bluffs and precipitous hills. These are covered with a dense growth of shrubbery, and all bearing thorns of one kind or another, forming what is called in the Mexican language, the chapparal. The immense stock which for ages had grazed upon these heights having kept down the grass, deep ravines have been washed out by the rains, rendering it, for the most part, a frontier easily to be defended.

We had passed below Reynosa, unable as yet to make any discoveries of particular consequence, when, one night, we were overtaken by one of those heavy fogs peculiar to that section. It rolled over us like a great volume of thick smoke, so dense as to close our vision against all surrounding objects. Stumbling on and on, we became confused and lost. As it began partially to disappear, we came suddenly upon two Mexicans, peons, watching their flocks. One of them was captured, the other making his escape. Inquiring of the prisoner where we were, he conducted us to a slight elevation, when to our astonishment we found ourselves in the very suburbs of the city of Matamoros; and learned further from him that the town was crowded with troops preparing, as he understood, to march against Texas. Well aware the Mexican who had escaped would report our presence, and not doubting that a troop of cavalry would presently be clattering at our heels, we turned our horses' heads and dashed back at a far greater rate of speed than we had advanced. However, we distanced all pursuers, if indeed any ventured a pursuit, and in due time once more crossed the Rio Grande, and encamped within the boundaries of our own state.

In the course of our travels, arriving at the Rio Frio, we espied a large party galloping towards us across the prairie, which proved to be the notorious Antonio Perez, with two hundred of his thieving vagabonds at his back. Thinking it scarcely prudent to encounter so large a force on the open plain, we fled to a narrow strip of timber on the riverbank, and there waited their approach, which was as rapid as their steeds could bear them.

The battle lasted for an hour and was quite as warm as those engaged in it thought either pleasant or convenient, and resulted in the enemy withdrawing, leaving us to pursue our journey undisturbed. In this battle, on the banks of the Rio Frio, we had one killed and several wounded, while the Mexicans left us numbering thirty less than when they approached. Nineteen times out of twenty a Mexican bullet passes as many feet above the object at which he fires. The philosophy of it I do not pretend to comprehend, nevertheless I know it to be the fact from no small experience, and this accounts for the disparity in numbers killed by the opposing parties, observable in these contests, for it cannot be denied that, generally, they are brave in battle.

At length, reining up our horses once more in the plaza of San Antonio, Hays dispatched a messenger to the commander-in-chief, with a detailed account of our long excursion, when, in order to recruit ourselves and animals, we were temporarily disbanded. Without delay, I hurried off to my old quarters on the Guadaloupe, where, for a long period, I passed away the time, alternately attending to business and indulging in the pleasures of the chase.

CHAPTER 5

The little town of Seguin, on the Guadaloupe, which, as before stated, I had selected as my abode, derives its name from Colonel John M. Seguin, whose extensive estate was situated on the opposite shore, and whose career occupies a large space in Texan history. He was a native Mexican, the son of Don Erasmo Seguin, a prominent citizen of San Antonio, and, like Antonio Perez, had once enjoyed the confidence of the Texan government, and like him, also, had betrayed it.

From this town I had gone down on some matter of business to Gonzales, thirty-six miles below, riding a mule instead of my favorite, the Black Prince, being desirous to preserve him in as fine condition as possible. Returning, I reached Seguin early in the morning, and on entering the town, at once perceived the whole population, my friends and neighbors, in the highest state of excitement. They were gathered in groups, or hurrying to and fro, everything indicating some unusual occurrence had taken place. I was not long in learning what in those times naturally suggested itself, that during the night the Mexicans had entered the place and stolen nearly every horse it contained, besides a large amount of other property, and with their proverbial cunning bad managed to make their escape without detection.

I mingled with the crowd and immediately became inspired with the prevailing indignation, for I was not long kept in ignorance of the fact that Black Prince, whom I regarded as the apple of my eye, had likewise been swept away with others in the general pillage. This was a loss I felt more deeply than the reader will probably be able to comprehend. Without wife or child, or any relative within a thousand miles, I made him my pet and companion, and though savage and dangerous to others, towards me he was gentle as the lamb. Many a night had we passed together out on the silent prairie. I had clung to him in the midst of enemies whose loud shrieks filled the heavens with the noise of war—long and bravely, over mountains and across the plains, he had borne me safely on his back—and who can wonder I came to think of him with genuine affection, regarding him more as an intelligent being than a poor dumb beast?

The day wore on until noon, the excitement still undiminished, when an object was discovered on the prairie as far distant as the eye could reach. It approached nearer and nearer, its outlines growing more and more distinct, until it assumed the shape of a horse coming at his utmost stretch of speed. Eagerly all eyes were turned towards him, and presently the crowd sent up the cry that it was the Black Prince. It was indeed him, and loud and hearty was the salutation he received as he dashed in among us, stopping by my side, panting for breath and covered with foam. He had evidently broken away from his captors, and ran from them as if conscious of the probability and danger of pursuit. For myself, on seeing him restored, I felt as one who, having lost his purse containing all he has, runs back and unexpectedly finds it in the path.

A party was now armed and organized, determined to follow the back track of Prince until the marauders were discovered. We followed it all day, and for a long distance, but finally struck upon the trail of a great drove of wild horses, where it was entirely lost, and further pursuit necessarily abandoned.

The following day I rode over to St. Geronimo Creek, six miles from Seguin. On this creek is situated the hacienda of the Nevarros, the most influential and wealthy family in that region, the head of which was then a prisoner in Mexico, having been taken with the Santa Fe Expedition. On the way I met Marcos Beremindo, the brother-in-law of the famous Bowie killed at the Alamo, and son of the old governor of Coahuila and Texas, under Mexican confederacy. During the wars his family had become reduced in its circumstances, and retired from Monclova, the capital of the provinces above named, to an indifferent ranche adjoining the Nevarros.

When I met him, he was on the way to Seguin to inform its citizens that Christolphe Rublo was in the neighborhood. He had learned from a garrulous Mexican that he had passed the previous night with his father, and that his band was secreted in a chapparal, twelve miles distant, halfway between St. Geronimo and St. Marks. I needed no further intelligence to confirm the suspicion already entertained as to who were the authors of the theft at Seguin.

It fell to my lot, in the course of a mysterious providence, to put Christolphe Rublo deliberately to death; and this fact furnishes me sufficient excuse for lingering briefly in the progress of this narrative to describe the manner of man he was.

He had been born and grew to manhood on the Nevarro estate, his father before him having from early life been its overseer. Under Mexican laws, he had passed, in the lapse of time, from the position of a citizen to that of a peon—a position differing but slightly from the condition of a slave. The difference is simply this—the latter, for a given consideration, may be passed directly from one owner to another, while the former can be transferred only by an assignment of the debt he owes. The redemption of a peon from his obligation, however, is an event far less likely to occur than a slave's escape from bondage.

From boyhood, Christolphe had been the terror of his neighborhood. He was possessed of an attractive person, and nature had generously endowed him with extraordinary talents, yet he was wanting altogether in every sentiment of morality. He was cunning as he was brave, treacherous as he was unscrupulous and implacable. His name had become synonymous with thievery and plunder, and there was no end to the stories of his daring and desperate adventures. At length, he crowned a lifelong infamy and filled to overflowing the measure of popular indignation by the commission of an unprovoked and wanton murder.

One of the most honored citizens of Seguin was an American gentleman by the name of Hance. During the harvest season he usually resided on his lands, a short distance from the town. On a quiet Sabbath day, while sitting alone in his country house, Christolphe Rublo stole to a window and shot him dead. Plundering the murdered man of his pistols and rifle, and mounting his saddle horse, he rode away forever from organized society, joining the roving band of Antonio Perez. Sometimes he would creep back to the hacienda of Nevarro on a stealthy visit to his father, who was not himself altogether unsuspected; nevertheless, he was thenceforward looked upon by the people of Seguin, and all the inhabitants for miles around it, as a robber and an outlaw, and, indeed, they were accustomed to hunt for him over the prairie, and in the timber lands along the rivers, as they would hunt for a ravenous beast, which, in fact, he was.

Partaking of the general feeling in regard to him, and having caught a due share of the excitement growing out of the recent robbery, I turned about, and as may well be conjectured, was soon proclaiming through Seguin the intelligence received from Marcos Beremindo. It was instantly resolved to raise a party to go in pursuit, but here a difficulty presented itself of a provoking character. With the exception of a fleet mare owned by one Milford Day, which escaped the plunderers, on account of having occupied an apartment in his dwelling house, there was not an animal, save a few old mules and broken-down Spanish nags, to be found in the whole place. It was impossible, therefore, to start a force sufficient to be of any service in such a chase as was proposed. Day and myself were the only persons provided with any sort of decent locomotion. Nevertheless, we concluded to set forth alone, and accordingly at early dawn next morning galloped away in the direction of St. Marks, on a journey of discovery.

We approached, at length, a dense chapparal, so dense as to obstruct the vision, surrounding entirely a smooth plat of ground, containing, perhaps, an acre. As we rode cautiously around the outer edge of this belt of shrubbery, Day suddenly halted, and placing his fingers to his lips as a sign for silence, pointed through a narrow opening. Looking through it, we saw within, ten or a dozen Mexicans with twice that number of horses, the party we were in pursuit of.

As a robber's retreat, no more admirable selection could have been made than this miniature prairie amidst the chapparal. A blind, narrow trail afforded ingress on one side, and a similar crooked path, egress on the other. Some of the banditti were mending their saddles— some repairing their moccasins and hunting shirts, while others were stretched upon the grass in apparent slumber. They were, evidently, unconscious that the eyes of an enemy were upon them.

We moved off silently to a thicket in the vicinity, dismounted, tied our horses in such a position as to avoid observation, and held a council of war. In the first place, the conclusion was unanimous and beyond question, founded on an unwavering confidence in the speed and bottom of our animals, that if pursued, we could easily outstrip them in a race. This point settled, we resolved not to retreat until they had received, from the muzzles of our rifles, at least one installment of the heavy debt which, in common with the plundered citizens of Seguin, we hoped eventually to liquidate entirely.

Returning to the chapparal on our hands and knees through the high grass, a favorable opening was discovered, not, however, until after a considerable search had been made.

Here we had a fair view of the party and much of the stolen property of ourselves and neighbors. For some time we watched them, anxious to distinguish among the group the form of Christolphe Rubio, but in vain. Nowhere could he be seen, yet we knew he was the captain of the band, and the cause of his absence was difficult to understand. If we could only secure him, alive or dead, we knew it would be a service the whole community would applaud, and which it had long and fruitlessly endeavored to accomplish; but the good genius which had attended him throughout all his murderous career, miraculously delivering him harmless from so many perils, still seemed to be enamored of his life, and to press close and lovingly to his side.

At length, becoming sensible of the imprudence of further procrastination, and that "delays are dangerous," we drew our rifles to the shoulder and fired. The report brought the whole party to their feet like an electric shock, and among them Christolphe Rublo, hitherto concealed behind a pile of buffalo skins and blankets. During the confusion thus suddenly created we discharged our revolvers, and then ran back to the thicket, mounted our horses, and made ready for a long, sharp ride, with the whole pack in hot pursuit. Instead, however, of beholding them as we expected, emerging from the chapparal and making towards us, we were utterly astonished on perceiving they had taken the opposite direction and were flying from us like frightened deer. Evidently they supposed us the advance party of a large force, and fled without waiting to ascertain the mistake. Indeed, such was the panic into which they had been thrown that, in their haste to fly, they left most of their saddles and much other property behind them. We entered their camp, taking as large a load of it as was convenient to carry, and returned to Seguin, destined, straightway, to enter on a new series of adventures far more tragical and exciting.

CHAPTER 6

The intelligence we brought back to Seguin, with the evidence of the captured saddles to corroborate our story, immediately aroused the town. Experience had taught us with infallible certainty that the party we had surprised and so singularly put to flight would hasten, without delay, towards the Rio Grande. In doing so they would necessarily cross the Guadaloupe, at the Seguin ford, a mile above the town, the Lipan ford, six miles farther up, or the San Antonio crossing, fifteen miles distant, the present site of the flourishing village of New Braunfels. It was, however, generally considered that, in all probability, they would direct their course towards the latter point.

Arrangements were made accordingly—the citizens marching out on foot to the lower ford, while a small party, as well mounted as the scarcity of horses, under the circumstances, would allow, proceeded to the upper crossing.

We reached it towards midnight and having carefully examined the white sand of the shore, discovered they had not arrived. Secreted in an ambush near by, we waited patiently their coming all the long night. In the morning, we determined to sally out in pursuit of them, but were scarcely seated in the saddle when they were espied at a long distance, coming towards us, across the prairie. Falling back out of sight, we silently awaited their approach, as long as concealment was necessary or politic, and then dashed upon them. Instead of turning back upon their course, they fled towards a belt of timber on the river bank three miles below, losing three men in the flight, and passing through it, plunged into the stream, seeking shelter on an island there situated. This island may be perhaps fifty yards in length, grown up with cottonwood, against which logs and brush have drifted down in seasons of high water, and lodged, forming a kind of breastwork. The space between the east bank and the island, which they crossed in reaching it, is narrow and shallow, but on the west side the stream is deep and rapid, and the shore, though neither rocky or perpendicular is high and difficult of ascent.

The Mexicans, when we came up, were concealed behind the breastwork of driftwood, but aware that a few minutes only would elapse before we would be upon them, plunged, one after another, into the stream, striking out towards the west shore. The strong current, in spite of their lusty efforts, bore them down the river, bringing them in range of our rifles. Three only escaped, one of these, sorely to our mortification and chagrin, being the ever fortunate Christolphe Rubio. And not only did he effect his own deliverance, but as if some magic power had turned aside the bullets that whistled round him, succeeded in partly dragging, partly coaxing his horse, the only one saved, up the embankment.

This horse was known as the Calahan pony, a round, tough, short-legged specimen of his race, and destined thereafter to figure conspicuously in the history of Christolphe Rublo. He was one of the number stolen at Seguin, the property of one Calahan, who, in order to make the assurance of his safety doubly sure, on the night of the invasion of the robbers, had placed a chain around his neck and fastened it with a padlock, the other end being passed through a hole in the door of his house and carefully secured within. Padlocks, however, offered but slight resistance to Mexican greed and ingenuity, and the astonished Calahan, in the morning sought to lighten the burden of his indignation by indulging in commentaries on the whole "magnanimous nation," far more profane than elegant.

Another who escaped enjoyed a reputation for villainy second only to Rublo. He was the son of a Roman Catholic priest who officiated in the ancient Cathedral of San Antonio. His mother was an obscure woman belonging on a neighboring ranche. Not allowed to bear his father's name, and not desiring to assume that of his mother, he came to be distinguished simply as the Ranchero, an appellation signifying, substantially, "the farmer." From a neglected boy, he grew up into a vicious vagabond, and following the natural bent of his inclinations, finally became renowned as a reckless and bold marauder. Though fortunate on this occasion in eluding his pursuers, he was doomed to bear away with him a ragged wound upon the shoulder. The third that escaped was unknown to fame.

Besides these three, another had crossed in safety and was out of reach of danger, but dropping his maleta, a sort of leathern haversack, while ascending the steep bank, with a foolhardiness unexampled, he turned back to secure it. Bending down to pick it up, a rifle ball crashed through his brain in the twinkling of an eye, bringing to the ground his brawny form, which rolled down and sank, with a great splash, in the river.

Afterwards one of our company swam over and secured the maleta. An examination of its contents disclosed three hundred silver thimbles, a number of silver butter knives, and several letters written by one Azaras la Ture, a French Mexican of Gonzales. This correspondence informed the party of Antonio Perez of the situation of a large number of horses in his neighborhood, and of the manner in which they could be stolen without danger of detection. It proved an unfortunate discovery for La Ture; the citizens of Gonzales, on inspection of evidence so conclusive, feeling constrained to relieve him from the further burden of existence by summarily suspending him from the limb of a tree. The silver knives and thimbles were ascertained to have been sold by a firm in Bexar to some traders going over to Mexico, and who were undoubtedly waylaid, robbed, and murdered on the way, as they were never heard of afterwards.

We had now succeeded in recovering all our stolen property, excepting the Calahan pony and one other, accidentally shot in the melee, besides having visited upon the offenders severe punishment. If we had been fortunate enough to have secured Christolphe Rublo, our labors would have been crowned with complete success. As it was, however, we directed our course homeward with the rescued animals, indulging a reasonable amount of satisfaction.

I was selected, as being the best mounted, to carry intelligence of our operations to San Antonio, the headquarters of the Rangers, and to notify them that Rublo was in the neighborhood. Leaving the party at the Lipan ford, I struck across the prairie, and leisurely pursued my journey. The excitement and labors of the two days past, together with the entire loss of sleep the previous night, now began to force upon me the absolute necessity of rest. At dusk, therefore, I dismounted on the outskirts of a grove, gave Black Prince a wide range to graze, and throwing myself on the ground, enjoyed a long and refreshing sleep. In the morning I continued on the way, reaching San Antonio somewhat before noon.

As soon as I arrived, I sought out Jack Hays, who cut short his salutation to tell me that Christolphe Rublo had been in the city that morning before daylight, and that he had just learned from a Mexican spy that he represented his party had been attacked by the Comanches in the mountains, from which only himself and two companions had escaped alive. Recounting to him all the particulars above related and the cause of my visit to town, we set about considering the best plan of accomplishing his arrest. Inquiries were everywhere instituted to ferret out his hiding place, until reliable information was finally received that he had gone down the river nine miles, and had taken refuge in the mission of San Juan, where he expected soon to be joined by a reinforcement. A party of some twenty was collected and started in pursuit. Arrived at the mission, we surrounded it, while Captain Hays and Colonels Howard and Cook were deputed to enter and seize the prisoners.

The mission of San Juan is situated near the bank of the river, and is surrounded by a high, thick wall. It is entered through massive folding gates, which open into a spacious courtyard, having been erected long ago after the fashion of old times, and had been used both as a safe retreat in war, and a quiet abode in peace, but latterly had become rather a den of thieves than a place of prayer.

Admission being demanded, the huge gates swung back, and Hays and his companions entered. They passed onward into the courtyard, and were received by the priest in charge, and disappeared in an adjoining apartment. At that moment Christolphe Rublo and the unknown Mexican who had escaped with him from the island darted out, the former running in one direction, the latter in the other. Aware of our approach, and intuitively comprehending the object of our mission, they had, with the notorious cunning of their class, stationed themselves against the wall, and as the great gate swung back, it concealed them from the observation of those who passed within. Rubio, in his flight, stumbled into a deep ditch, which had been excavated for the purposes of irrigation, and was speedily captured, while his companion plunged into the river under a sharp fire, and swam to the other shore. The report of firearms brought out the workmen in a gristmill, just below the point he had succeeded in reaching, on seeing whom he recrossed, making directly towards the spot where I stood, with great difficulty, and evidently suffering intense pain. I took him by the hand and drew him out upon the bank, presently discovering he was unable to stand upon his feet, having a fractured thigh. He was carried into the mission and left in charge of the Holy Fathers who presided over it, while Christolphe and his comrade, the Ranchero, who was found in bed, suffering from his shoulder wound, were conducted back as prisoners to San Antonio.

Entering the city, we were surrounded by the populace, who clamored for their blood. With the utmost difficulty we were enabled to protect them, but finally succeeded in confining them in the office of the alcalde, which, however, was defended by a guard. Jack Hays announced, and in a manner which meant precisely what he said, that any man who laid violent hands upon the prisoners in the city of San Antonio would do so at the forfeit of his life, but pledging his word they should be forwarded to Seguin, in charge of the Rangers, to be dealt with by the outraged citizens of that town as they might think proper to determine.

When this announcement was made, the great body of the populace demurred, saying, in the first place, it would be unsafe and imprudent for the Rangers to leave the city unprotected, and in the second, that unless the robbers were guarded on the way by such an escort, they would certainly be rescued by the many secret adherents of Antonio Perez. Hays, however, apparently adhered firmly to his expressed determination, communicating privately, however, to one Escue and myself, the plan he had resolved on—a plan which will be developed as we proceed.

Two hours before sunset, Rublo was bound fast upon the back of the Calahan pony, which we had also captured at San Juan, and the Ranchero on an old Spanish gelding, whose hobbling gate and decrepit aspect indicated beyond mistake he had well-nigh traversed the last quarter of his life. The Rangers, therefore, were called out and ordered into line. They left the city, led by Jack Hays, taking the road leading toward Seguin, Escue and myself leading the animals which bore the prisoners, in the rear, and in this order we journeyed onward to the Salado ford.

Just before reaching this point, however, agreeably to a previous understanding, we fell back a considerable distance from the main body, and turning to the right, silently led the prisoners out into the plain, guided by no trail, but steering as near as possible in the direction of Seguin. Hays, thereupon, wheeled about and marched back to San Antonio, the object of these maneuvers being to prevent both the rescue of the prisoners and an attack upon the town.

It was some time after nightfall when we separated from the Rangers at the Salado ford, yet we took the precaution to wrap ourselves and captives in dark buffalo skins, in order that we might not be discovered, even in the darkness. We soon realized the advantage resulting from this foresight, inasmuch as we could plainly discern numbers of Mexican horsemen in their white shirts scouring the prairies round us, while we remained unobserved. As night advanced it began to rain, and the darkness became intense. We reached at last, the bank of the Cibilo, having accomplished in safety the first half of our journey, but here we became confused, and considering the danger of an attempt at crossing at random, resolved to halt until morning.

Removing Rubio from the pony, I bound him firmly, and sat down by his side with a pistol in my hand. I knew well the unpleasant reception that awaited me at home—that it might cost me as much as my own life was worth—should the prisoner escape through my neglect; and consequently determined not to close my eyes through the night. Before falling asleep, which he did at last, the hardened desperado, conscious that his deliverance, on the morrow, into the hands of the men of Seguin would close his mortal career, boasted of the many outrages he had committed— his robberies and murders—and grinding his teeth, spit upon his enemies, and bade defiance to the terrors of death and the torments of hell.

Escue, with his charge, had chosen a spot whereon to pass the night some rods distant from me, alleging it afforded better pasturage for his horse. Ranchero complained bitterly of the pain in his wounded shoulder, and begged piteously that his arms might be unloosed in order to relieve him. His request was finally granted, and drawing his sombrero over his eyes, and nestling between two buffalo skins, he sank into an apparent slumber.

Escue tied one end of his long cabalos, or halter, round his horse's neck, the other end to his ankle, resorting to this measure for two reasons: first to restrain his horse within proper limits, and second, believing the action of the halter on his ankle would keep him awake. But Escue for some nights back had "murdered sleep," and withal, during the day, had partaken somewhat freely of his beloved whisky; wherefore, as the night wore on, and the exhilaration passed away, a sense of drowsiness pressed down his eyelids with a force more ponderous than he was able to resist. Several times through the night I spoke to him, in a voice loud as prudence would permit, and roused him from his napping.

The first faint light of morning disclosed to me, as I looked in his direction, that something was out of place. I could not discern his horse, though perhaps it might be in consequence of an intervening cluster of bushes. "Is everything all right, Escue?" I called out in a half-doubting tone. Drawing up his leg, he felt the halter was still fastened to his ankle, and looking down, beheld Ranchero's hat, to all earthly appearance with his head in it, and answered, "all right." "But are you sure?" I continued. This second interrogatory opened wide his eyes, when, raising the buffalo robe, his face assumed the expression of complete astonishment, as if the voice of an invisible thimble-rigger was whispering in his ear, "You see, my unsophisticated friend, the little joker is not there!"

A moment's further investigation was sufficient to inform him that his horse had mysteriously vanished also. The other end of the halter instead of encircling his neck, was fastened to a musquete limb which admirably counterfeited the motion of the horse, as it swung to and fro. The cunning Ranchero had performed this feat in a manner the shrewdest juggler might, indeed, have envied. The first point gained was the liberty of his arms, which enabled him to untie the cords that bound his feet. Seizing, then, the favorable moment, he slipped away, leaving his hat undisturbed, the buffalo skins naturally separated by upright sticks—and tying the cabalos to the limb, moved off with the horse, noiselessly as a cat. For some time Escue stood dumb with astonishment, but when the faculty of speech returned, he declared the feat was utterly unparalleled, inasmuch as his eyes had been on him constantly from the moment he lay down, and swore, if he ever had the good fortune to meet him again, he would treat him with the awe and reverence due to a supernatural wizard.

The sun was fairly risen before we were ready to proceed. I had placed Rublo astride the Calahan pony, his arms firmly pinioned, and was in the act of securing his feet, when, turning my eyes towards the prairie which gradually ascended as it stretched back from the spot we occupied, I beheld, perhaps a mile distant, a company of horsemen. A brief period sufficed to enable us to distinguish our stolen horse in advance of the troop, with Ranchero on his back.

A critical moment had now arrived. Not the fraction of an instant was to be lost. Escue was without a horse—the old Spanish gelding being utterly useless under the circumstances. To retain the prisoner was impossible, and to release him would be to set free a remorseless bloodhound, and to bring down upon our heads the anathema of the community. He sat upon the pony, with outstretched neck, gazing intently towards the rapidly advancing horsemen. An eager, sinister, half-malicious, half-triumphant expression overspread his countenance, suggestive of the certain presence of a devil. My resolution was instantly formed, and instantly executed. Drawing a revolver from my belt, I shot him. As he tumbled heavily to the ground, Escue mounted to his place, and before the smoke of my fire had evaporated in the air, we had plunged down the bank into the river, at this point wide and deep, and were pushing, for the love of life, to the farther shore.

On reaching the river, the pursuing party was subjected to a brief delay. We improved the time, as we best could, to accomplish our escape, but had not proceeded over three miles when we again discovered them in the rear, slowly but surely gaining on us. I had no apprehensions for myself, knowing Black Prince could easily bear me far beyond their reach whenever called upon, but I could not forsake Escue, whose short-legged pony, though a willing and persevering little beast, was utterly unable to meet the exigency of the occasion.

Thus situated, but one resort with any prospect of success occurred to me. Wheeling suddenly about when they had reached a dangerous proximity, I drew my rifle to an aim. The movement brought the party to an instant halt, Escue, in the meantime, urging the pony forward by every possible appliance in his power. Practicing this maneuver many times, my rifle reaching much farther than their clumsy muskets, as they soon became aware, we finally reached the vicinity of Seguin, when they abandoned the further prosecution of the chase. Ranchero's escape from Escue was fortunate, but this pursuit, so far as he was concerned, terminated fatally, indeed. A force of thirty men sallied out of Seguin on our arrival, overtaking his party on the Santa Clara, where, in a fierce encounter, he brought to a brave conclusion a turbulent and reckless life. It may occur to the reader, as he peruses these passages in my history, that they contain much which is cruel and unnecessary. In the midst of peace—protected by law—with none to molest or make him afraid—he will probably fail to comprehend the precise situation of a Texas citizen during the stormy period of which I write. Nevertheless, he should bear in mind that Texas then was passing through that sanguinary struggle which led to her independence—when she was surrounded and threatened on all sides—when the land was overrun with robbers and murderers who spread everywhere desolation and death, and who utterly laughed to scorn the authority of law. Comparatively few in numbers—with tribunals powerless to protect him—he had no other alternative than to return blow for blow, and to demand blood for blood.

CHAPTER 7

At the time of the plunder of San Antonio in March 1842, by the forces under General Rafael Vasquez, I was absent in the Red River country, but again joining the Rangers in the course of the summer, was one of the party who first discovered the approach of General Woll's army in the autumn of that year. This discovery was made by four of us while ranging, as spies, down the Medina River. Woll's army consisted of some twelve hundred Mexicans, entering Texas through an unfrequented quarter, cutting their way through chapparal thickets hitherto regarded as impassable, and which, to this day, is distinguished as General Woll's trail.

We brought the intelligence of their advance to San Antonio, but it was barely delivered when Woll's proclamations arrived, promising impunity to all who should be found in the peaceful performance of their civil duties, but threatening, with the most condign punishment, those who should be overtaken with arms in their hands. These proclamations divided the inhabitants of the city into two opposing parties—one advocating submission, the other resistance. Among the former, was the court, then in session, Judge Hutchinson presiding, with a large circle of lawyers round him. Their determination exerted a prevailing influence, much to the dissatisfaction of the Rangers, who knew that, for themselves, they were beyond the pale of mercy or forgiveness. They made their arrangements accordingly, first securing their horses in a grove beyond the river, near the Alamo, and then carrying up stones, with which they built a breastwork on the paved roof of the office of the alcalde. Just before daylight, with banners flying, and a great flourish of trumpets, Woll's army entered the town; our little band, in the meantime, pouring in among them a continual shower of lead, until, approaching within twenty feet of us, we leaped down from our position, fled across the river, mounted our horses, and without the loss of a man, scampered away to the banks of the Salado.

The report of the enemy's arrival at San Antonio reached Gonzales the same day, when the citizens, to the number of eighty or one hundred men, under the command of Captain Matthew Caldwell, joined us by the way of Seguin. From other quarters our number was increased to, probably, three hundred. The night succeeding our retreat, several of us conversant with the Spanish language went back to the outskirts of the city where a drove of their cavalry horses were grazing. Passing the drowsy sentinels in the guise of herdsmen, replying to their challenges in their own tongue, we cut their hobbles and quietly retired. Bestriding our horses, left at a proper distance in the rear, we dashed in at full speed among the unfettered mustangs, whooping and yelling like incarnate fiends. The result was that the drove stampeded, as also did the sentinels—drums beat, and trumpets sounded in the town, but we galloped back to camp, a goodly number of the frightened mustangs preceding us.

Next day, the Rangers, headed by Jack Hays, myself acting as lieutenant, were sent out for the purpose of drawing the Mexicans into an engagement. We continued to advance until we reached the Alamo, when the enemy's cavalry, several hundred, approached us. As directed, we fired upon them, and then fell back upon Caldwell's position, who had now assumed command, where the Texans lay in eager expectation to receive their enemies.

They were not long kept in suspense. Woll, with the vanity peculiar to his country, saying, "he would go in person and drive the Texan wolves from the bushes," marched forward with nearly his whole force. Caldwell was well posted, among the timber, behind the bank of Salado Creek. The action commenced at eleven o'clock and continued until nearly sunset. It was a hot and bitter fight, the particulars of which I omit recording, as not properly coming within the scope of personal narrative. Yet, the spirit which animated "Old Paint" on the occasion, the name by which Caldwell was distinguished, will be seen in his first report of the engagement, of which the following is a copy:

SUNDAY, September 17, 7 o'clock, P.M.

At the Salado, two miles above the old crossing, we commenced fighting at eleven o'clock today. A hot fire was kept up till about one hour by sun, when the enemy retreated, bearing off their dead on the ground, and very many dead and wounded were taken from the field by their friends. We have a glorious band of Texan patriots, among whom only ten were wounded, and not one killed. The enemy are all around me, on every side; but I fear them not. I will hold my position till I hear from reinforcements. Come and help me—it is the most favorable opportunity I have ever seen. There are eleven hundred of the enemy. I can whip them on my own ground without any help, but I cannot take prisoners. Why don't you come? Huzza! huzza for Texas!

Woll retreated to San Antonio, surrounding and massacring on the way a party under Captain Dawson, and then hurriedly set off for the Rio Grande, taking with him, as prisoners, Judge Hutchinson and twenty-one others, clerks, lawyers, and jurors—the captives receiving little sympathy from the Rangers in consequence of the servile welcome they had extended to their captor. They were conducted to the city of Mexico, subjected to many indignities in the course of their long and tedious march—but finally restored to liberty through the intercession of the American consul.

This invasion of the country, and the atrocities with which it was accompanied, led to the famous "Expedition to Mier." What is to be done? was the question. Shall this system of outrage be forever practiced upon us with impunity, and a hundred miles' flight screen the invaders from punishment? It was everywhere asked. These questions were deliberately considered, and resulted in a universal resolve to carry the war into the enemy's country. Appeals were sent abroad for volunteers, and were answered promptly from all directions.

President Houston, though apparently yielding to the popular demand, was, nevertheless, at heart, opposed to the project. I rest this statement principally on the fact that about this time I was sent by Jack Hays with dispatches to the Executive, then at Washington-on-the-Brazos, informing him of the recent movements of the Rangers and of the general feeling of the inhabitants in the west. Houston sent me forward to Galveston with instructions to the authorities to prevent volunteers joining the expedition, and ordering them to repair the defenses in the vicinity of that city. Notwithstanding these instructions, however, when my mission was fulfilled and I departed on my return to San Antonio, twenty of the citizens of Galveston accompanied me, among them Colonel Walton, the mayor of the town.

Reaching Columbus, we found a large number of citizens assembled at a barbecue, gotten up for the purpose of raising volunteers. General Burleson was present, the man almost unanimously called upon to lead the proposed expedition, but superseded for reasons best known to the President, by the appointment of General Somerville to the command. General Houston, beyond all question, at least in my own mind, was thoroughly opposed to the project now in contemplation; nevertheless, he scattered over the country a flaming war proclamation, calling upon the first class of drafted men from many counties to rendezvous at Bexar, to pursue the enemy into Mexico, chastise him for his insolence, and concluding by expressing the hope they would call to their lead a man of valor, wisdom, and experience. Such a man was Burleson—the enthusiastic choice of the volunteers—and yet Somerville, in whom they had no confidence, was appointed in his stead. This proceeding I account for only on the supposition that General Houston, wishing to float down smoothly with the current of popular opinion, determined to frustrate finally the whole affair by committing it to the direction of one over whom he exercised unlimited control. Subsequent events abundantly confirm this supposition.

At the end of September, volunteers to the number of twelve or fifteen hundred had pressed forward towards the San Antonio River, all eager to follow the enemy and punish him on his own soil. Five weeks after the barbecue at Columbus, Somerville arrived from his Custom House office at Matagorda Bay and took command. The forces were scattered around Bexar, at from one to ten miles distant, occupying some six or eight different encampments. Instead of concentrating, organizing, and drilling his men, the General sat down quietly in the town for two weeks, receiving the hospitalities of those very persons who had been foremost in entertaining General Woll. This brought about the last of November, and with it cold rains and cutting north winds, as uncomfortable to the poor men lying out on the open prairie as the General's quarters in the city were cosy and luxurious.

What was murmur and dissatisfaction before, against Somerville's operations, now became loud and bitter denunciations. Many believed nothing would be effected under him, while others were indignant at not being provided with those absolute indispensable munitions of war— powder and lead—which were known to be in the town of Bexar, and to have been freely tendered to General Woll, and which we could easily have obtained from its hostile citizens. The consequence was that great numbers returned home, angry and disgusted.

A force, six or seven hundred strong, however, still remained, and on the eighteenth of November concentrated at the Presidio crossing of the Medina. They were then within five days march of Woll's retreating army, which had halted to give them battle. The men were anxious for the fight, and had Somerville moved promptly forward, there is not the remotest doubt the entire Mexican army would have been captured.

The six or eight days, however, the Texans lingered at the crossing of the Medina, in the absence of their general, were well improved. Most of them had left their homes during the warm, genial days of September, with raiment too thin for the sharp November weather; and now in the absence of a military clothing establishment, industriously occupied themselves in transferring deerskins from the backs of their natural owners to their own. Deer abounded in great plenty, and hundreds of them were slaughtered daily, the camp presenting, more than anything else the appearance of a vast tan yard. At length the General arrived, and orders were issued for immediate march.

Hays' Rangers, including myself, with fifteen Lipan Indians as guides, preceded the main body. In the progress of the march, the little army found itself struggling and plunging through a "post oak bog," and all who are acquainted with the nature of a post oak region after a heavy rain will readily conceive the difficulty of its passage. This kind of land, with much appearance of firmness to the eye, and in fact, sufficiently firm to bear the weight of an ordinary-sized man, will not sustain a horse. Two days were employed in advancing the distance of five miles over this deceptive region, presenting during the whole time a scene ludicrous beyond description. All over the prairies as far as the eye could reach, horses and pack mules were floundering and plunging; some with their legs entirely out of sight, their noses resting quietly on the ground— others lying on their sides, afraid to trust their pedal extremities under them—coffeepots flying in one direction, and frying pans in another, while their owners indulged, some in curses and some in laughter, according as their various tempers prompted.

At length, however, early in December, we reached Laredo on the Texas side of the Rio Grande, which was evacuated by the Mexicans on our approach, who retired beyond the river. The authorities of the place provided us with a few beeves and a scanty supply of provisions when we were ordered to march down some three miles below the town, where we encamped. The next day, being in a suffering condition for want of provisions, dissatisfaction became loud and determined. The men declared that if their general would not furnish them with the necessaries of life, they would furnish themselves, and accordingly several hundred marched into the town and helped themselves. This was "the plunder of Laredo," about which so much ado was made by the partisans of General Somerville, and which was subsequently given as one of the reasons of his abandoning the expedition.

Once more the army took up its line of march, moving in a tardy, zig-zag course, winding about in the chapparal, but eventually reached the river opposite the city of Guerrero, distant six miles from the other shore and directly in front of an Indian village at the mouth of the Rio Salado. Had General Somerville, instead of adopting the course he did, promptly crossed the river at Laredo and swept down the main road with a celerity befitting the occasion, he would, in all probability, by this time, have taken every town as far down as Reynosa; but here he openly avowed a determination which, it was more than suspected, he had all along entertained. On the morning of the nineteenth of December he issued an order commanding the troops to march at ten o'clock for the junction of the Rio Frio and the Nueces, thence to Gonzales, and there disband. Captains Fisher, Cameron, Eastland, Ryan, and Pierson refused obedience to this order, together with three hundred men, of which I was one. Somerville with two hundred officers and privates, however, set out on his return, reaching Bexar in January, while the other party having elected Captain William S. Fisher to the command, resumed their march down the river, transporting their baggage, provisions, and a portion of their troops in several flatboats captured at the mouth of the Salado—and on the twenty-first encamped opposite the town of Mier. Ben McCullough, myself, and several others were dispatched, in the capacity of spies, to reconnoiter and ascertain if troops were in the neighborhood. We entered the city and learned that Canales had just evacuated it, but that other troops were hourly expected. On the morning of the twenty-second a requisition was made upon the alcalde for provisions and clothing. He readily promised the articles demanded should be delivered at a specified point on the river below the Texan camp. That day and the next, however, passed away, but still the requisition was not filled. In the meantime our spies had captured a Mexican who reported that General Ampudia had arrived at Mier and prevented the fulfillment of the alcalde's promise. Thereupon, our forces resolved to pass the river and give them battle.

We entered the town about two o'clock in the morning in the midst of a drizzling rain and in total darkness, driving the enemy before us. Advancing to a street leading directly to the square, we found it protected by artillery. The course then adopted was to take our position in the street, fire upon the artillery, and then, turning hastily round the corner, reload, while the enemy's grapeshot passed harmlessly by. Thus the night wore on, when, in order to protect ourselves from the inclemency of the weather, we commenced opening passages through the stone houses, until we succeeded in advancing within fifty yards of the artillery. Portholes were then opened and a destructive fire kept up. When daylight appeared, so that we could see the artillerymen, the unerring Texan rifle soon silenced their pieces. The Mexicans then clambered to the housetops and the fight continued, having now been carried on in one form or another for nearly twenty hours.

At length, Colonel Fisher, in repelling a charge, was wounded. During the confusion caused by this event, the Mexicans sent in a white flag by Dr. Sinnickson, one of the Texas prisoners they had taken, with a proposition from General Ampudia for us to surrender, declaring we should be treated with all the consideration due to prisoners of war; that we should not be sent to Mexico, but kept upon the frontier until peace returned, or an exchange could be effected, and that if these terms were not accepted we should be allowed no quarter. Our commander believing it impossible to reach the east side of the Rio Grande without a loss of at least two-thirds of his surviving force, concluded, finally to surrender upon the terms proposed. The enemy had engaged in this contest over 2,000 men; the Texans, 261. Our loss was sixteen killed and thirty or forty wounded, while the Mexican loss, though never definitely known, was doubtless as many as five hundred.

At the time of the surrender, myself and ten others had become separated from the main body and had taken refuge in a house in the southern quarter of the town.

The firing having ceased for some time, I sallied out, and looking round a corner, saw our men marching into the square without arms. Running back, I informed my comrades that the troops had surrendered, but expressed, at the same time, the determination to die rather than go to a Mexican prison. Without lingering to deliberate upon the matter, I leaped out of the back window and hastening down a long garden, crawled in under a chapparal fence thickly overgrown with weeds, securing a position that hid me perfectly from observation. A path ran within a few feet of me, over which Mexicans were constantly hurrying back and forth, exultingly shouting to each other that the Texans were taken, and heaping upon them maledictions without number.

Here I remained until after dark, when cautiously venturing forth, I made for the Alcantra, a small but rapid stream, in a bend of which Mier is situated. Passing it in safety, I pushed forward with the utmost diligence, striking the Rio Grande half a mile above the point at which our troops had crossed. Here all was darkness and silence, and though my prospects were gloomy enough, indeed, I could not repress a feeling of exultation, and a deep sense of gratitude to Heaven at my escape thus far.

Divesting myself of apparel, I tied it in my handkerchief, fastening the bundle on my head; my rifle I bound on my back, the breech extending above the shoulder, secured my pistols and bowie knife in my belt, and plunged into the river. The object of this arrangement was to keep dry the lock of my rifle, my clothes, and powder—a very plausible thing in theory, but as experience taught me, impossible in practice. The river here was wide, and the night so dark, I could but faintly distinguish the opposite shore. For a long time I buffeted the waves, the bank on the other side appearing to recede as I approached. Strength began gradually to give way—I felt I could hold out but a very little longer. Fortune, however, favored me; hope bore me on and up, as the bold outline of the shore became distinctly visible; now it was five rods distant, now two, now one, now, with a great, last effort, I had reached it, but alas! only to find it a high perpendicular bluff, whose clammy, slippery side, offered not the slightest thing for me to grasp. The water beneath me was deep—myself exhausted—there seemed to be no prospect whatever of relief, and as I floated down the tide, throwing out my hands against the remorseless rock that mercilessly beat me back, I regretted that some friendly bullet at Mier had not saved me from such a dreadful death.

Drifting on and on, in utter hopelessness and despair, I floated, at last, against a treetop which had been blown down, and whose branches, as they spread out upon the water, were to me the arms of mercy stretched out for my deliverance. With just sufficient strength to seize them, I succeeded in reaching the shore, and found myself in a narrow ravine, which here ran down to the waterside. After much exertion and suffering many bruises, I reached the height above, covered with "prickly pear," whose needle-like thorns tore my flesh at every step as I pushed my way through them. At last, I came to an open space, perhaps twenty rods long, free from the tormenting briars that surrounded it. At either end were two large trees, rising far higher than their species usually attain, standing there, stiff and silent, like two great sentinels.

My clothes, notwithstanding the precaution I had taken, as well as the powder carefully packed within them, were of course saturated; a chill "norther likewise was blowing at the time, so that the idea of sleeping in my present plight was out of the question. On the contrary, in order to create warmth, of which the weather and the water had deprived me, I ran across the open space from one tree to the other; passing the entire night in this manner.

My reflections, as the reader will readily divine, were not at all of the most encouraging character. I was sufficiently conversant with the country to be aware that, between the lonely spot to which fate had mysteriously brought me and the settlements on the Nueces stretched a wild and dangerous region of more than a hundred miles. I could have attempted its passage, however, with a resolute heart, had it not been I was destitute of ammunition, which not only deprived me of the means of procuring an existence, but of defending myself against attack. For aught I could then exactly comprehend, I had only escaped slaughter at Mier, and a watery grave in the Rio Grande, to be again either recaptured by the enemy or starve to death on the prairie.

Indulging contemplations such as these, I discovered, about sunrise, a column of smoke, at the distance of a mile, curling lazily above the chapparal. It first occurred to me that perhaps it proceeded from the fires of the Texan guard, which had been left on this side of the river, in charge of our horses. Making towards it immediately, and as fast as possible, I soon ascertained my supposition was incorrect. Instead of our guard, they turned out to be a brace of Mexican herdsmen in charge of a large flock of sheep and goats. One was a man, apparently forty years of age, the other an effeminate, slender strippling of nineteen. As I discovered them, they were near a thicket, on the border of an extensive prairie, a couple of mules grazing near them, and their guns leaning against a tree. They were at breakfast, evidently relishing their coffee and tortillas and little dreaming of interruption. Keeping the bushes between them and myself, I crawled up through the grass, unperceived, almost within a dozen yards of them.

I had confidence, growing out of some considerable experience of Mexican character in trying emergencies, that I could, with proper energy, overcome and capture them both. At any rate, let the result be what it might, I resolved to attempt it. Accordingly, taking an unloaded revolver in one hand and a bowie knife in the other, intending to knock one down with the pistol and dispose of the other with the knife, if resisted, I rushed upon them with a yell that made the welkin ring. Both dropped upon their knees and screamed lustily for quarter. I commanded the oldest one to lie down on the grass, which command he instantly obeyed, and still presenting the pistol, ordered the youngster to bind him. This complied with, I secured the latter, and then cleaning my rifle and revolver and loading them with their ammunition, sat down beside them, and while devouring with most ravenous appetite the unappropriated tortillas, discussed affairs as they then existed, and speculated generally upon the prospect of matters and things in future.

My first inquiry was whether they knew the trail to Casa Blanca, and being answered in the affirmative, proposed that if they would guide me thither, their lives should be spared. They gladly acceded to the proposition, though begging earnestly that the boy might be released. This request was respectfully though emphatically declined. I now tied them upon one of the mules, took possession of their guns and ammunition, killed and dressed a sheep which I bound upon the back of the remaining mule, and mounting in the rear of it, gave the order to march. Preceded by the captured herdsmen, who proved to be peons, and the most ignorant of their class, I journeyed three days, over a country as wild and desolate as can be imagined. During all this time I did not once close my eyes in sleep. Halting at night, I ordered them to dismount, watching beside them as they slept, pinioned on the ground. The carcass of the sheep furnished us with food, thereby enabling me to avoid attracting the attention of any roving band of Mexicans or Indians by shooting game. The poor herdsmen were in a constant state of alarm, assuring me over and over again they would not mislead the "Buena Americana," yet I well knew the cunning rascals would take my life whenever an opportunity presented.

During the afternoon of the third day, as we reached the summit of an elevated piece of ground, Casa Blanca was distinguished far in the distance. I now fully comprehended my situation, being familiar with the geography of the country we had reached, and no longer needed the services of a guide. The prisoners had faithfully fulfilled their promise, and it only remained for me to fulfill mine. I dismounted, placed one of their guns against a tree, and beside it the larger portion of their ammunition, particularly calling their attention to the spot, and then proceeded on our journey in our usual way, four or five miles. Here I unbound them, and having exchanged salutations, we separated, both parties, to all appearance, mutually satisfied The object of leaving the gun and ammunition so far behind was that I might dismiss them unarmed, a precaution I considered necessary; and that they, also, securing them on the return, might have the means of killing game for their support on the long journey back.

After parting with them, I hastened onward several miles, by this time greatly exhausted, and turning into a thicket, lay down to sleep, four nights having now elapsed without a moment's rest. My purpose was to proceed next morning before break of day, but when I awoke, the sun had passed the meridian, and was shining down full upon my face. I awoke in extremest pain—my limbs swollen—my brain on fire—and suffering that deathly sickness which seemed the forerunner of certain and speedy dissolution. With great difficulty I managed to mount the mule, and succeeded in reaching the ranche of an old acquaintance named Corlies, whose kind attentions restored me to comparative health, when I pressed forward to San Antonio, bringing the first intelligence of the disaster at Mier.

CHAPTER 8

Having made a flying visit to New Orleans after my escape from Mier and accompanied the Rangers on several excursions, particularly on one occasion to Comanche Peak, above Austin, I returned once more to Seguin, and entered upon my old occupation of trading in horses and cattle. In the years 1844 and 1845, I frequently drove large herds from western Texas to Fort Jesup in Louisiana, for the use of the American army.

On one of these occasions, having arrived with a considerable drove in excellent condition, as I supposed, a portly officer met me near the fort, gruffly demanding if it was my intention to poison the army of the United States by furnishing them such carrion, and without allowing me time to reply to the imputation, continued to heap upon me the most violent epithets the English language afforded. I was so taken by surprise, and his abuse was so unmeasured and unreasonable, that I lost my temper, and placing my hand upon my pistol, threatened, unless he "shut up," to shoot him. Thereupon, he turned suddenly on his heel and walked away with a grin on his face, not exactly in consonance with the terrible wrath he had just exhibited. Presently Charley May approached me, inquiring what I had been about, saying General Twiggs had just sworn that that Texan cattle drover had no more sense than to shoot a man. This announcement somewhat startled me, and my astonishment increased when an orderly advanced with the information that General Twiggs requested my presence at his quarters. With a good deal of reluctance I complied, fearing I had committed some serious blunder, but was received with the utmost cordiality and handsomely entertained. He smoothed over our encounter in a laughing way, and learning I had long been a Texas Ranger, interrogated me closely and minutely in regard to the towns, rivers, and general nature of the country on the Rio Grande. He likewise conducted me to General Taylor, to whom I repeated all and more than I had previously stated, and finally departed in the best possible humor.

Soon after this occurrence, the army under General Taylor moved forward to Corpus Christi. The war breaking out between the United States and Mexico, Jack Hays was ordered to raise a regiment of mounted Rangers. I was among the first to join him. Before the regiment was filled, a party consisting of eighteen, myself among the number, under command of Captain Walker, otherwise known as "Mad Walker," had permission to go forward in advance. Arriving at Corpus Christi, we found that Taylor was at Fort Brown, surrounded by the Mexican army under General Ampudia, and cut off from his supplies at Brazos Santiago. Leaving Corpus Christi, we rode across the country towards the American camp, a distance of 140 miles or thereabout, resolved to reach it in one manner or another. Within eight miles of the fort we came in sight of the Mexican forces extending entirely across the prairie. A consultation followed among us touching the best method of getting round them, when Walker, to our infinite surprise, coolly announced he was going through them. It was sometime before we could realize he was in earnest. Such a foolhardy attempt struck us all, except Walker, as utterly impracticable and absurd. Nevertheless, one after another avowed he would not be behind his comrade in anything, let the consequences be what they might, until all had fallen in with the proposition of their commander.

Accordingly we advanced, approaching the Mexican line in an ordinary walk. We were dressed in such a manner it was impossible to distinguish us either as Texans or Mexicans. Doubtlessly they supposed we were a party of their own countrymen—coming to join them, or messengers bringing some intelligence. It was evident they had no suspicions whatever, for, though all of them were looking directly at us, they stood carelessly with their arms at an order. Still we continued to advance slowly and silently, not a word was said, until, having approached within fifty yards, the word was given to charge. Instantly the spurs were buried deep in the sides of our good horses, which bounded forward like the wind, and greeting them with a terrific yell, we dashed right through. In their efforts to get out of the way, "Greaser" tumbled over "Greaser" in a comical disorder, and such was their astonishment, we were suffered to pass 150 yards before a shot was sent after us, and then without effect.

Coming in sight of Fort Brown at a rapid gallop, a party of dragoons sallied out to ascertain what our approach might signify. Waving a white handkerchief, we rode up to them, and were escorted to the fort, where General Taylor, in a manner too expressive of astonishment ever to be forgotten, greeted us with the exclamation, "How in God's name, boys, did you get through?"

Our little band of eighteen was now attached to May's dragoons, as spies, in which capacity we accompanied that division of the army which marched over to Point Isabel, and on its return with the provision train, first discovered the Mexican forces, drawn up between the lake and chapparal, in the pass of Palo Alto. During the whole night following the engagement which took place we were out reconnoitering, and brought back to General Taylor intelligence of the enemy's position at Resaca de la Palma. In that bloody contest which ensued, we participated in the charge led by Charley May, which resulted in the capture of General La Vega, and silencing the battery of the enemy.

After this victory Hays' regiment arrived, and remained with Taylor from the time he left Matamoros to the storming of Monterrey. To that regiment, during this period, I was attached. A description of the march from the former to the latter place, recounting with any degree of particularity the incidents that occurred, would fill many volumes larger than this narrative is designed to be. The services of the Texas Rangers, in common with the entire army of which they formed a part, during this memorable epoch, constitutes a portion of the enduring history of the country, with which the world is sufficiently familiar. I shall allude to it no further than to say that throughout all my experience in war, I have seen nothing that could be compared with the long and terrible battle of Monterrey. Years have rolled away since that event occurred, yet the ghastly corpses that filled its streets still haunt my sight, and the groans and shrieks and agonizing cries for water and for mercy of its wounded and dying men are still ringing in my ears.

The term of service for which the Rangers enlisted had now expired, and most of them returned to Texas. At this time Colonel Hays visited Washington and received permission to raise another regiment of a thousand men, to serve an indefinite period. Once more I joined him at San Antonio, from whence we set out to join General Scott in Mexico. It was a long journey, extending through the heart of the enemy's country more than five hundred miles. The region traversed by us was generally wild and uncultivated. We crossed some mountainous districts, though the route led principally over vast, undulating tablelands. At remote distances we passed haciendas, stock ranches, covered with thousands of horses, sheep, and cattle, literally far exceeding in number those possessed by that patient patriarch of old who dwelt "in the land of Ur."

The science of agriculture is little understood among the scanty population which inhabit this territory. Manufactures are almost totally unknown; the nearest approach to it I witnessed was the making of blankets by the women, which are woven on the ground with sticks, somewhat after the manner of knitting. The people are a mixture of Mexican and Indian, ignorant, indolent, and filthy, a tortilla, a roasted squash, a little boiled milk, and now and then a curdled cheese, and string of beef dried in the sun comprising their ordinary diet.

And yet there is not a land more fertile, or a climate more delicious on the earth. With such cultivation as is bestowed on our northern soil, it would be capable of sustaining incalculable numbers. If ever the time shall come when internal strife and contention shall cease in that distracted land—when a system of education shall be established, and a wise and stable government be maintained—when industry shall take the place of indolence, and the energies of her people directed to the development of her resources, instead of spending them in the commission of robberies and the promotion of civil war. I see not why Mexico should not become the paradise and garden of the world.

We were six weeks on the route, during which time we had many skirmishes with roving companies of guerrillas, and at last encamped eight miles outside the town. A company of dragoons met us here and escorted us in, our army at that time being in possession of the capital.

We were some nine hundred strong, and perhaps no body of men ever presented a rougher or more ridiculous appearance than we did on that occasion. The thorny chapparal of the plains had torn our garments into shreds, and we had not shaved in six weeks. The accumulated dust of travel lay thick upon us, giving evidence our baggage mules had not been burdened with the weight of clothes brushes, or if they had, that they had been marvelously neglected. Withal, our horses were kept back at the point the escort met us, in order to preserve them in condition for service, so that we were constrained to ride upon pack mules, little long-eared jacks, scraggy Mexican ponies, and whatever of the kind we could most conveniently secure for the occasion. Thus mounted, with uncombed hair— ragged and unwashed, we made our grand entrance into the conquered city of the Montezumas.

Intelligence of our approach preceded us. The sidewalks were thronged with thousands of men, women and children, all anxious to obtain a sight of the dreaded Texas Rangers, of whom their countrymen, returning from the battles of the far frontier, had said so much. They were plainly disappointed in their expectations. Instead of inspiring them with awe, our appearance only excited their contempt and risibility. All the batteries of their wit were discharged upon us, even the little boys hooting and the women laughing in derision. At length they carried their jokes to the extent of pelting us with dirt and pebble stones. One tall fellow in the crowd, who had rendered himself so conspicuous as to attract particular attention, finally threw a brickbat, which happened to hit a Ranger named Bill Stewart, who was mounted on a jack. This was more than his temper or philosophy, under the circumstances, could enable him to withstand. The brickbat had scarcely reached its mark before a bullet from the muzzle of Bill's revolver, laid the Greaser on his back. The next minute, Tom Hall, farther in advance, disposed of another in like manner, and for similar cause. Our further progress was entirely undisturbed.

Reaching the south side of the Grand Plaza of Mexico, we reined up and dismounted. Presently an American officer approached and inquired for Colonel Hays. I pointed him out, when, moving forward a few steps and looking at the youngster in old clothes I had designated, he returned, remarking it was the colonel of the regiment he desired to see. I assured him the person I pointed out was that gentleman, when he again stepped forward and informed him the General wished to see him directly. At Hays' request I accompanied him. Entering General Scott's quarters, he raised his apology for a cap, saying, as he did it, "Colonel Hays, at your service." Scott measured him from head to heel for some time, and at last replied with a stern manner and in a rough voice—"I hear your men have commenced a career of murder in the city. I hold you, sir, responsible." With the utmost coolness Hays replied, narrating the circumstances above stated, and though entirely respectful, both in manner and language, conveyed the idea that whatever responsibility might be imposed upon him, if Mexicans thought proper to indulge in the amusement of throwing brickbats at the heads of the Rangers, any different result from that complained of need not be for a moment anticipated. The truthful straightforward statement of the affair at once mollified the brave old chief, and a pleasant conversation ensued, during which he inquired particularly into the condition of our men and animals, and dismissed us with the assurance our services would be speedily called into requisition.

The city at this time was crowded with American troops, the brave men who had fought their way within its gates exhibiting a gallantry and courage such as we rarely read of in the chronicles of war. In a short time we joined the Second Dragoons under Colonel May, and were ordered out to pursue Santa Anna, then a fugitive in his own country. It was a long and exciting chase. We rode chiefly at night, allowing our horses to graze, and sleeping ourselves during the day. Frequently we galloped eighty miles between the setting and rising sun, over mountains, through swamps, across the plains, wherever the hardy guides might lead. It was a hunt on a grand scale, and very often did we almost run down the wily fox of which we were in pursuit.

On one occasion we came so close upon him that in his haste he dropped his wine horn, which was discovered by a Ranger from the Colorado. It was made of an enormous ox horn, and held precisely a gallon. In the bottom was screwed a silver cup, and the stopple so arranged as to lock. It was beautifully and elegantly finished, richly inlaid with silver, which was engraved "Antonio Lopez de Santa Anna." At the time we found it, it was half-filled with wine. The Colorado Ranger brought it home to Texas, where it yet remains, among the curiosities in the museum of Galveston.

At last Santa Anna surrendered himself to General Scott, and by him was ordered to be safely conducted from the country. He came to this determination, unquestionably, through fear of the Texas Rangers. When he found they were in such hot pursuit and that escape eventually was impossible, he knew there was no other alternative. There would have been no quarter for him had he been captured, for among us were men who thirsted for his blood—men of the Mier and Santa Fe expeditions, who, through his instrumentality, had lingered in loathsome dungeons and worn servile chains, and who would have shot the tyrant wherever they might have encountered him, in any place and under any circumstances.

The surrender of Santa Anna rendered the further services of our regiment unnecessary, and consequently we returned to San Antonio in a body and there disbanded. This terminated my career as a Texas Ranger. The lessons which the Mexicans had been thoroughly taught by our army were too impressive to be forgotten, and thenceforward peace and quiet prevailed along her borders. The Indian tribes retired to their haunts among the mountains of the unknown north. By the act of annexation, the lone star of Texas, which had so long twinkled faintly in the political firmament, and which, like the star in the east, had guided her early patriots, was enabled to burst through the clouds, and assume its place in the glorious constellation of the Union. The wild excitement of border warfare was at an end; the necessity which called out her citizens, bristling in arms for her defense, was passed; and Texas was left, unmolested, to fulfill her destiny, which, in my humble judgment, is to become the richest and most powerful state in this confederacy.

CHAPTER 9

With the return of peace, my thoughts began to revert to old times and old friends from whom I had been so long absent, and who were unaware whether I was dead or living. Accordingly, I resolved to leave Texas for a season, in order to gratify a desire of seeing them once more. Taking passage at New Orleans, I ascended the Mississippi to St. Louis, crossed from thence to Chicago, and eventually arrived in my native county of Jefferson, on the shore of Lake Ontario.

I pass over in silence the greetings and congratulations that awaited me on meeting the surviving members of my family, who had supposed for years that I was dead. I presented myself before them as one risen from the grave. They listened with inquisitive and untiring curiosity to the long story of my adventures, while I, in turn, made inquiries concerning the friends and playmates of my youth, some of whom had grown to manhood and still lingered on their native soil, while others had been gathered to their fathers and slept beneath it.

Here I remained a year, but the coldness of the climate, during the winter months, affected me injuriously, rendering it necessary, for the preservation of health, to terminate my visit. I returned to Texas, by the same route previously traveled, stopping at Galveston, San Antonio, Seguin, and finally halting at Corpus Christi. I was now engaged for several years in my former business of trading in horses and cattle, during which period nothing of peculiar interest occurred.

While following this pursuit, in the year 1855, I became acquainted with a man named William Aikens, an energetic, intelligent, enterprising person, who had been a resident of Bastrop on the Colorado, but had lately arrived from California through the Indian country. He had conceived the project of purchasing a drove of mules and horses for the California market, representing they could be driven through in safety and confident it would prove a profitable speculation. Not having sufficient means of his own, he proposed the formation of a joint company, and inasmuch as I had much experience in stock buying, he earnestly solicited me to unite with him and others in the undertaking. The company was accordingly formed with a capital of seven thousand dollars. The following were the proprietors: William Aikens; Thomas Martin, of San Patricio, formerly of Philadelphia; John Stewart, a Scotchman of San Antonio; John Smith, of Seguin, a native of Ohio; William Smith, of Gonzales; Henry Jones, of Huntsville; Robert Hall, of Crockett; and myself. Aikens was acknowledged as leader or captain, and, together with myself, undertook the general superintendence and direction of the enterprise.

We made our headquarters at first at San Patricio, on the Nueces, thirty miles above Corpus Christi. Before commencing operations, Aikens and myself visited New Orleans, where we purchased arms, ammunition, blankets, saddles, tents—in fine, an outfit sufficient to furnish twenty-seven men, the number of which our company, proprietors, and subordinates, consisted. While picking up these supplies, I discovered accidentally one day, a large silver watch, of such unusual and extraordinary dimensions as to attract attention. My curiosity being excited, I requested of the shopkeeper the privilege of examining it, and found it to be an alarm watch, one, likewise, that would make a far louder and longer racket than any I had ever before seen. It could be regulated so as to "go off" at any required moment, and so powerful was its internal machinery, it would move across a common table whilst ringing the alarm. It occurred to me that such an article would be of signal service on our proposed trip, and I, fortunately, purchased it at an expense of forty-five dollars. I am thus particular, for the reason, as the reader will hereafter see, that this watch has been closely connected with my destiny, and to it I am indebted for life and liberty this day.

Returned to San Patricio, we hired nineteen assistants. The agreement we entered into with each of them was that he should accompany us on the trip to California, rendering such services as circumstances reasonably required, and remaining with us until the drove was sold, in consideration of which he was to receive his horse and equipage and fifty dollars in money. In order that their unhappy fate may be known, should this volume fall into the hands of any of their surviving friends or relatives, I here insert their names, with such limited information relative to their antecedents as I possess: They were Henry Hall, brother of Robert, one of the company, a lad about seventeen years of age; Andrew Jones, from Mississippi; Benjamin Howard, formerly of Mobile; William and John Haynes, brothers; Peter Shaw, of New Braunfels; William Hand, of Corpus Christi; Barney Campbell and Peter Hickey, both Irishmen from New Orleans; Augustus and Adolphus Voss, cousins, from Victoria; Walter Scott, from some town on the Trinity River; Andrew Hempstead, a French Canadian; John Adams, from Philadelphia; Amos Sand, an eccentric Yankee, hailing from New England; and Amos Jordan, an Englishman. Besides these sixteen, we had engaged three Mexicans to act in the capacity of horsebreakers. They were Juan Gazzier, of Corpus Christi, Antonio de Silva, of Saltillo, and Martinez Ferrarez of Matamoros.

With this company, well mounted, and fourteen pack mules, we left San Patricio and set out directly for the city of Matamoros. Our plan of operations was to start northward from this point, collecting our drove as we advanced. This was in March, a month in which vegetation is rank near the mouth of the Rio Grande, and it was further our intention to proceed leisurely, keeping within the latitude of its healthy growth; in other words, to use a familiar expression in that quarter, especially among those engaged in similar enterprises, "to follow the grass." From the adjacent ranches, as we moved along, passing to the left of the river towns, we collected such animals as we deemed advisable to purchase, so that on our arrival at San Fernando, a frontier town some forty miles westward of Fort Duncan, our means were exhausted, and our drove had increased to the number of 395. From San Fernando we moved forward, leaving civilization behind us at the little settlement of San Augusta, and pushed on diligently in the direction of Paso del Norte, aiming to penetrate the gorges of the mountains, until we should strike the California trail. We traveled slowly, at the average rate of fifteen miles a day, it depending entirely upon the distance between watering and feeding places. At none other did we encamp.

After leaving the settlements, it was our established custom to sound the bugle at half past three o'clock in the morning. All hands then aroused, some going out to "round in" the drove—some packing the mules, others busied in preparing breakfast, consisting of the broiled flesh of deer, bear, or buffalo, with coffee and hard biscuit, but always without any kind of vegetables whatever. These repasts were prepared in rude camp kettles, our plate being simply tin cups and bowie knives; nevertheless, gathered around the fire on prairie grass, we satisfied the cravings of appetite with a zest unknown to dyspeptic people. Usually we "dined," &c., in the open air, but in seasons of very rainy weather, we ate and slept under a tent, much, however, to the disgust of the mule drivers who had charge of them, and who regarded such luxuries as superfluous and absurd.

Breakfast over, we moved forward briskly, at the word of command, a squad of five or six invariably moving a considerable distance in advance, in order to look out for Indians and prevent a stampede. An occurrence of the latter character was especially dreaded, and provisions were made accordingly to prevent it. Very many, undoubtedly, will not comprehend precisely the meaning of this term. Over the prairies of the Southwest, thousands of mustangs, or wild horses, are roaming constantly. If, in their course, they happen to come upon, and mingle with, a drove of their own kind, the latter, however gentle, seem instantly to change their nature from a domestic to an untamed state, and flying with their wild companions, are rarely seen or heard of more. Such, in the language of the prairie, is a stampede.

Behind the advance party some half a dozen mares were led, having bells, usually the common cowbell, suspended from their necks, and on each side of the drove rode horsemen in single file, the remainder of the party with the pack mules bringing up the rear. We generally halted about noon, resting until the next morning at half-past three. While resting, especially during the night, the men acted alternately as sentinels whose duty was to ride constantly round the camp. In this manner, day after day, we moved on, crossing wide valleys and winding through ravines and mountain passes, sometimes following the course of streams, at others toiling directly over precipitous heights, burying ourselves at last far within the depths of that wild and mountainous district, situated, as near as we could determine, 350 miles northwest of Eagle Pass. In our progress, when we came to a river it was necessary to cross, our manner of proceeding was as follows: The animals carrying the bells were taken over, when their leaders would commence shaking the latter violently. The drove grazing on the other shore would immediately erect their ears, look intently a while in the direction from whence the sound proceeded, move to the water's edge, and if the bank was high, run up and down the stream in an agitated mood, finally plunging in, however deep or rapid, and swimming to the other side. "Bell mares," as they are styled, are indispensable, therefore, on occasions of this kind. On the march, I witnessed many demonstrations of the fact that there is a charm the most obstinate mule is unable to resist in "the tintinnabulation of the bells."

On the last day of March we entered an enchanting valley, five miles wide, perhaps, and twenty long. It was surrounded on all sides by high mountains, covered with cedar. Here and there were little groves of musquete and oak, nearly through the center flowed the clear and crystal waters of a narrow stream, alive with innumerable speckled trout. Scattered in various directions over the luxuriant surface of the valley were antelopes, deer, buffalo, and wild horses, some grazing, others standing lazily in the shadow of the oaks. In this spot, so pleasing and attractive to the eye, affording such an abundance of grass, and such conveniences of wood and water, we determined to remain six weeks, or rather until the foaling season was passed. The weather was bright and pleasant through the day, the nights cool and foggy. Having resolved to remain here so long, our tents were erected with more care than when making a temporary halt. We gathered wood, prepared a fireplace, and made every arrangement for comfort that circumstances would allow. With little to do save preventing the drove from straying, we anticipated that, with fishing and hunting, the time would pass agreeably away.

The second of April was remarkably fine—the air was balmy and delicious—the sun shone gloriously. From early in the morning I had been in the saddle, riding up and down the valley, sometimes distant ten miles from the camp, ascertaining its capabilities of furnishing forage, and whether there were wild horses in the neighborhood. In the evening we gathered around the camp fire, each broiling his buffalo steak, which the skill of Antonio de Silva, the horse breaker, had furnished, or frying brook trout taken from the adjacent stream, while the boys amused each other with narrations of many a frolicsome adventure. The whole party was in excellent spirits, lying down to rest on their buffalo skins, when the meal was over, laughing and joking, and singing snatches of familiar songs.

It was my watch that night until twelve o'clock. Going out I rode about the camp, chatting with the other sentinels, and at midnight came in with them. John Haynes and his brother William, Barney Campbell and Augustus Voss taking our places. At this time everything seemed to be in proper order; there were no indications of danger or disturbance from any quarter, though it had grown quite chilly and an intense fog was gathering. Taking off my coat and folding it, I laid it down on the buffalo robe to serve as a pillow—set my watch so that the alarm would strike at precisely half-past three, the usual hour of rising, and placed it under the coat, and then lay down, outside the tent, under the branches of a low musquete tree, near the fire, drawing a heavy Mexican blanket over me. I did not fall asleep immediately, pondering in my mind whether the grass would be good upon the mountains by the time we should be ready to proceed. All my companions, however, had sunk into profound slumber. Not the lightest sound disturbed the deep silence that prevailed, except the distant tinkling of the horse's bells, which occasionally came faintly to my ear. At last, about one o'clock, perhaps, I dropped asleep.

Was it a dream? Was it a real shriek that rang out upon the air? The first moment of awakened consciousness was sufficient to assure me that it was indeed reality. Springing to my feet, I discovered at once that the camp was full of painted and yelling savages. Seizing the rifle which always lay on the buffalo robe by my side, I drew it to my shoulder, knowing well there was no chance or hope of safety, but in desperate resistance, at any and whatever odds. Before I could collect my thoughts, however, at almost the instant I arose, a lasso, that is a rope with a noose on one end, was thrown over my head, jerking me violently to the ground. Half a dozen Indians sprung upon me, some holding down my arms, others my legs, another astride my body with his hand upon my throat. When I had been thus overcome, they tied my feet together, and bound my hands behind my back with stout thongs of buffalo hide, using far more force in the operation than necessity required, and drawing them so close as to cause me severest pain. All this occurred, probably, within the space of five minutes. Of course, I was greatly confused, not so much, however, as to be unable to comprehend the dreadful situation I was in. My knowledge of Indian character and customs, gathered from the lips of an old frontiersman in Texas, taught me that perhaps three or four of us might be spared to figure in the accursed rites of their triumphant war dance, but whether I was to be reserved for such a purpose, or destined to be slaughtered on the spot, was a matter of terrible conjecture. With as much composure as was possible, in such trying circumstances, I awaited anxiously the issue.

CHAPTER 10

I soon became aware that the only members of the party who escaped the massacre, which proved to have been bloody as it was sudden, were Thomas Martin, John Stewart, Aikens, and myself. The first two had been secured much in the same manner I was, but Aikens, who was sleeping in a tent, had succeeded in escaping a short distance, and had engaged in a hot scuffle, during which he fired upon his assailants before he was overpowered. The first step taken by the savages, after the confusion had subsided, was to strip us of every particle of apparel, and clothe us in their own fashion of dress, which consisted simply of buckskin leggins, with a hunting shirt of the same material fringed at the bottom, and at the cuffs, and tied in front with strings.

While they were stripping and dressing me in this manner, one of them picked up my coat and discovered the watch. He seized it with avidity, examined it intently, turning it over and over, immensely pleased, as his countenance plainly indicated, with the singular and pretty bauble. While thus regarding it, the minute hand ticked round to half-past three, when the alarm went off. The utter astonishment of the Indian was beyond description. Holding it out at extreme arm's length, his head thrown back, and staring wildly, he was too much surprised, as it roared and rattled for two minutes, to decide whether it was safest to let it fall to the ground or retain it in his grasp. By the time it ceased, a dozen had gathered round him, looking into each other's faces in silent wonder. The one who held it presently pointed to me, then at the watch, then at the spot where he had found it, speaking at the same time fast and earnestly, informing them, I suppose, that I was the owner of it. Approaching and holding it out to me, they made signs expressive of their desire that I would cause it to repeat the alarm. The idea at once flashed upon my mind, that I might make it serve a useful purpose. They untied my hands—when I accepted it with an air of reverence and adoration, wound it up solemnly, and so regulated it that in a few minutes off it went again, and again was the dusky crowd struck with increased wonder and astonishment. This was repeated frequently, the savages in the meantime holding it to their ears to hear it tick as they had seen me do, when the chief wrapped it carefully and tenderly in his deerskin pouch and placed it in his bosom, not, however, until I had comprehended from their gestures, such as pointing upwards, then at the watch, then at myself, that they regarded it as something supernatural which connected me with the Great Spirit.

Their next step was to collect the plunder. In this, they were, indeed, thorough. Not only did they gather up all our buffalo skins, Mexican blankets, rifles and revolvers, culinary utensils, and the like, but the dead bodies were stripped to the last shred, and tied on the backs of their mules. Nothing was left behind. By this time the morning light began to break on the eastern mountains, and preparations were made to depart. Before starting, however, they unbound our feet, conducted us through the camp, pointing out the stark corpses of our butchered comrades, who had lain down to sleep with such light and happy hearts the night before. The scene was awful and heartrending beyond the imagination of man to conceive. Not satisfied with merely putting them to death, they had cut and hacked the poor, cold bodies in the most brutal and wanton manner; some having their arms and hands chopped off, others emboweled, and still others with their tongues drawn out and sharp sticks thrust through them. They then led us out some three or four hundred yards from the camp and pointed out the dead bodies of the sentinels, thus assuring us that not one of the entire party had escaped. The bodies of the sentinels were lying close together at the south side of a thicket, which suggested to me the probable reason of our being surprised before an alarm was given. The night, as I have said, was chilly, and instead of riding round the camp at proper distances from each other, as was their duty, they had undoubtedly huddled together under the thicket, in order to protect themselves from the cold wind that swept down the valley. In this position the Indians had crept up unperceived through the fog, and dispatched them so suddenly there was no opportunity to make an outcry. Beyond question we had been watched from the mountains ever since our arrival in the valley—indeed, I learned as much from them afterwards—so that they had plenty of time to deliberate upon the plan of attack. Before leaving Texas, I had insisted upon taking with me a favorite watchdog, but Aikens was confident he would prove only an annoyance, and I was persuaded, though reluctantly, to leave him behind. Had I adhered to my purpose, his vigilance, peradventure, might have saved us, for though they numbered between two and three hundred, I have no doubt we could have repelled them, had we stood on the defense and been prepared to receive them.

During all the time they were thus exhibiting the result of their savage work, they resorted to every hideous device to inspire us with terror. They would rush toward us with uplifted tomahawks, stained with blood, as if determined to strike, or grasp us by the hair, flourishing their knives around our heads as though intending to take our scalps. So far as I could understand their infernal shouts and pantomime, they sought to tell us that the fate which had overtaken our unfortunate companions not only awaited us, but likewise the whole race of the hated white man. All the dead, without exception, were scalped and the scalps, still fresh, were dangling from their belts.

This sickening and frightful ceremony ended, dressed deerskins were thrown over our heads, drawn down over the face, and tied with a string, closely about the neck. "We were thus completely blindfolded, and would soon have suffocated, had not a small hole been cut through the skin, under the nose, and in front of the mouth, sufficient to admit air necessary for respiration. We were then each mounted on a mule over an Indian saddle without stirrups, our hands tied behind us at the wrists, our feet brought as near together as possible under the body of the animal and firmly lashed. In this situation it was possible for us to roll off sidewise if we pleased, but it was impossible to extricate ourselves from the beasts.

The caravan set forward in the following order: Our drove in advance, with outriders in front, and to the right and left, guarding it in the same manner we had previously; behind the drove rode the warriors, and in their rear came the pack mules, and the mules bearing the prisoners, without bridles, but left to follow at their own leisure and discretion. It is customary, not only with the Indians on such occasions as this, but with Mexican and Texan drovers on a long march, to leave their pack mules free to follow, and never do they stray out of the line or linger many rods behind. Our position, bound as we were, however, was not comfortable. Utterly powerless, so far as guiding the animal was concerned, which, like the wind, wandered where it listed, sometimes pushing and crowding in among the pack mules, sometimes suddenly stopping to take a bite or two of grass, and in that natural and innocent act, throwing us forward on the pommel of the saddle with the impression we were going over his head, the next moment starting suddenly on a sharp trot, throwing us as far backward—our predicament was indeed awkward as it was tormenting. But these were only the light afflictions and trials of the prairie. When our journey came to lead us through strips of timberland, as it often did, then the measure of our tribulation was full, indeed. The first time the thoughtless brute ran under a limb, striking me in the face and knocking me off, or rather turning me round so that my head reversed positions with my feet, the sensation produced was horrible, but practice makes perfect is a true adage, and, in time, habituates a man to almost anything. My frequent repetitions of this performance on the tightrope rendered me an adept in this sort of somersault. There was one consolation attending it, the moment I went over, the mule would invariably stop, and an Indian as invariably run and right me up again.

Unable to see, I was in perpetual suspense. If the mule happened to be traveling at a sharp pace on these occasions, and the branches strong, it became a violent and serious affair, not only to the extent of inflicting great pain, but of endangering life. As it was, my face and breast were sorely bruised, resembling more the appearance of a pugilist returning from some Long Point than the ordinary features of a man. It afterwards afforded the Indians most excellent sport, a subject for infinite jest, and every performance was treated with "tremendous applause." No comic actor ever so amused his audience. Indeed, I could tell sometimes from the laughter that would begin to arise that danger was near, and lying close on the mule's neck, escape it. It was aggravating beyond endurance, converting any humbler emotions I might have entertained to those of uncontrollable wrath. If each malediction I bestowed on the high cheek-boned, copper-colored demons, and which came from the bottom of my heart, had possessed the weight of a grain of mustard seed, the whole Comanche nation would have soon been attending to their own torments instead of mine, in another and a hotter world.

About noon of the first day's march, the cavalcade halted, repacked the mules, roasted some venison, and after an hour's delay proceeded on the journey. At dark they again stopped for the night. When permitted to dismount, and the blindfold had been taken from my eyes, I discovered we were in a narrow ravine, a lonely and secluded spot, with high precipitous mountains rising close on either side, and near a large spring which gushed from a rock, the source of a considerable rivulet. The cords were here unloosed from my wrists; nevertheless, I was pinioned back from the shoulders, leaving my arms so far at liberty, however, that I could raise my hands to my mouth. The drove properly herded, one or two horses were shot, and the meat brought in for supper.

I may as well state, in this connection, that horseflesh is the favorite food of a Comanche Indian. They do devour great quantities of venison and buffalo meat, but these are universally considered as greatly inferior to the steaks cut from the carcass of a mustang. The woods and prairies are covered with wild fowl, and the streams abound with delicious trout and other fish, yet none of these are ever made use of as an article of diet.

A fire was now kindled, and the warriors gathered round it, the prisoners in the center. This was the first opportunity I had of seeing and speaking to my fellow captives. Martin was silent and dejected, apparently absorbed in his own reflections, and little disposed to converse. Stewart was nervous and frightened, bewailing his hard fate in tears; but Aikens maintained a cheerful spirit, advising us to keep up our courage and look the matter coolly in the face until the last. While conversing, the Indians were engaged boiling their meat, which they ate without any accompaniment whatever, save water dipped from the spring in buffalo horns; the greensward serving as their table spread, and their fingers as knives and forks. Having satisfied themselves, they now seemed to take into consideration the appetites of their captives.

In wandering menageries, the curiosity of civilized assemblages is sometimes excited to see "the animals fed in the presence of the audience." Something of this kind actuated the Comanches on this occasion. At all events, they resolved to make their disgusting horseflesh serve the double purpose of supplying us food for the body, and themselves food for mirth. In our Indian dresses, which consisted of leggins rising only to the knee, and a short hunting coat, the upper portion of the leg, that is, above the leggin, was necessarily bare. As we sat upon the ground together, our feet tied, it was likewise necessarily exposed. When the meat designed for us had boiled until the fat began to fry and sputter, they would throw it with such marvelous dexterity from the end of their roasting sticks, that it would fall on our naked limbs hissing hot. If the laziest reader of this book will try a similar experiment on himself, he will find it admirably calculated to arouse his activity. I venture to affirm he will squirm more energetically, turn over quicker, and throw a greater amount of exercise into a given period than he ever did before in his life. It had the same effect on us, and the muscular demonstrations we made during the exhibition "brought down the house" far more uproariously than any of our previous performances during the day. It resulted in my declining supper altogether, having a prejudice against the waiters in attendance, and of raising broad blisters on my person, the scars of which I will carry with me to the grave.

At the conclusion of these exercises, so refreshing on one side and so painful on the other, the warriors threw themselves on the ground to sleep. They lay near each other, forming a large circle, leaving a space in the center some fifty feet in diameter. Our sleeping apartment was in this space, and we were "put to bed and tucked up" in the following original fashion: First, we were made to lie down upon our backs, with our arms and feet extended. Four stakes were then driven firmly through the sward, to which our hands and feet were fastened, holding us in such a position that they were as wide apart as possible. Then two other stakes were driven close on either side of the neck, and a strong strip of buffalo hide tied from one to the other, so that it passed under the chin, across the throat. Thus we lay upon our backs, unable to move head, hand, or foot.

I had now tasted nothing, save a little water, for nearly twenty-four hours, yet was not hungry; had undergone hardships rarely endured, yet was not weary; my excited imagination had driven afar off the desire for rest or for refreshment. During the long watches of the night, my brain was busied with ten thousand fancies; but through the maze and shadow of them all, I could not see the remotest prospect of deliverance. I gazed up into the sky —I could gaze nowhere else—and wondered how it was that the good God who dwelt above the stars, omnipotent as He was just, could permit such a wrong as I was suffering to be perpetrated in His sight. Thus the wretched night, without having for one moment closed my eyes, passed off. The warriors, at length, bounding to their feet and preparing with much bustling preparation to commence the adventures of another day, to end—I knew not where.

The second day of the march, about midday, we reached a wide river—(I have since learned it was the upper Rio Grande, separating that portion of Mexico in which we were captured from the vague and unknown region of country distinguished on the map of northwestern Texas as the Presidio.) Here we were subjected to considerable delay. There was a large number of animals to be crossed over, besides a great amount of what they regarded, and which in fact was, valuable plunder.

At the point of the river where we reached it, was a low, long gravelly beach—a high, perpendicular rocky bluff directly opposite—but a mile below the bluff was another gravelly beach, almost precisely similar to the one at which we had arrived, and opposite that, and below us, was likewise a high bluff, so that in crossing, it was necessary to move in a diagonal direction, as well as a long distance. The usual labor was expended, and the usual means resorted to in passing the drove, which, in consequence of the low water extending from the opposite beaches, left only the main channel, a distance, perhaps, of a hundred yards, to be swum. When it came our turn to take passage, the blindfolds were removed, and each was seated in a little buffalo-skin boat, an invention original, I believe, with the Comanche tribes, and capable of being taken apart, folded into a small compass, and carried as baggage. To the bow of these boats were hitched one end of a hair rope, the other to the tails of our mules, who safely ferried us from shore to shore.

That night we encamped at the foot of the mountain, and the whole of the next day traveled, as near as I could judge, over a steep, rough, and uneven road. During the entire trip, I was subjected to the same annoyances of being run under trees, burned with hot horseflesh, and staked down at night, as described above.

Early in the afternoon of the fourth day the warriors raised the war whoop, and afar off was heard another war whoop in reply. As we advanced, over what appeared to me a smooth plain, the answering voices grew more and more distinct, until finally the approaching parties met and intermingled. Having halted, I was taken from the mule, and when allowed the liberty of my eyes, found myself and companions standing together, in the midst of a great number of tents, and surrounded by five or six hundred men, all pushing forward to catch a glimpse of us.

Some little time elapsed, when the crowd gave way, forming a passage through which advanced the leader of the war party, accompanied by an aged chief and a squaw, the latter the only one of her sex then anywhere to be seen. Having reached us, the watch was produced and handed to me, with signs indicating they wished me to exhibit its marvelous qualities.

It became me now to put forth all my histrionic powers, and to feign emotions far different from the real ones that were struggling in my bosom. My object was to take advantage of their credulity and superstition to establish among them the notion that it was a thing of life— a spiritual medium, having powers of speech—through which their chiefs and prophets, and great warriors who had gone to the land of spirits, could converse in a language perfectly intelligible to me, but utterly incomprehensible to them; to indoctrinate them into the solemn belief that my old "turnip," as I usually called it, was no less than the brother or offspring of the sun, and on such intimate and familiar terms with him, that it could foretell through me the precise moment he would reach any given point in the heavens, and that such was the unity of feeling existing between them that the short second hand of the watch, in its lesser sphere, kept corresponding pace with him as he went round and round the world. Finally, and most especially, to imbue their minds with the importance and solemnity of this one great truth, that connected as the watch and myself were, both with the visible and invisible world, any mishap that should befall either would inevitably disarrange the machinery of universal nature, break a cogwheel, or something of the sort, and send us "all to smash."

The character it became necessary for me to assume, therefore, was that of a missionary, expounding my peculiar doctrines among the heathen. Accordingly, I received it at their hands in an attitude of great humility, and gazed upon it with that air of reverence which may be supposed characterizes the Hindoo kneeling before the graven image of a monkey, wound it up, held it to my ear, listened to the tick, tick, tick, with a solemnity of expression intended to convey the same idea, as if I had said to them in their own language: "Gentlemen Indians, I am now receiving important telegraphic dispatches from the other side of Jordan!" Presently, it sounded the alarm. It would have been a curious and interesting picture for an artist, could he have watched the various expressions of astonishment, awe, and wonder that overspread their features during the whir and whirl and whiz of the cunning mechanism. Ejaculating their impressive "ugh, ugh," they looked seriously and inquiringly into each other's faces, as much as to say— "Well, I never; did you ever!"

Finally, the watch was taken by the old chief and formally presented to the squaw, whom I afterwards learned was his favorite wife. The presentation speech I was unable to understand, but surmised it was very similar to those which usually accompanies the presentation of flags in more civilized communities, that is to say, an exhortation to the recipient to stand by it until the last drop of blood has been spilled, and to preserve it, under any circumstances, "sacred and inviolate." This ceremony over, I was conducted to the chief's tent, regaled with a late dinner, horseflesh being the only dish mentioned on the bill of fare, and this without the useless luxuries of salt and pepper, and very rare, when I was seated at the entrance, and had a brief opportunity of taking a view of the town.

This Indian village, in every material respect, was like other Comanche villages with which I afterwards became acquainted, and a description of it in this place will suffice for all. It consisted, I should say, of four hundred tents, and covered a space of six or seven acres. In the center of the village was a capacious square, perhaps one acre, and in the center of the square stood a lodge, the largest in the town, being the business tent of the civil chief. Around the square the wigwams were arranged with great particularity. Leading into it on the four sides were regularly laid out streets, the tents standing in line on both sides. Those of the principal men were the largest, and fronted the square; those of their inferiors, according to their rank, diminishing in size, and extending backwards.

The tents are constructed of prepared buffalo skins, the flesh side outward, and, from a distance, an Indian town like this, to the eye of a white man, is novel and attractive. The manner of their construction is as follows: Poles, from ten to twenty feet in length, are driven diagonally into the ground in the line of a circle, at the distance of three or four feet from each other, and at such an angle that their tops will nearly meet. These poles serve the purpose of rafters over which the buffalo hides, firmly sewed together, are drawn and fastened by stakes on the ground, thus forming an impervious cone. The door does not turn on hinges, but is simply an extra pelt, fastened at the top, with a heavy weight at the bottom, and which, when raised or turned aside sufficiently to admit an entrance within, falls directly and closely to its place. Around the outside is dug a narrow and deep ditch, rendering the floor dry and hard, and the smoke of the fire, which is always kindled in the center of the wigwam, escapes through a hole at the apex. These villages are always located near running water, and in thinly timbered groves, which break the force of the north winds in the wintry season, and in hot and sultry weather shade them from the sun.

I had remained in the chief's tent but a short time when I was again conducted to the square. There I found Aikens, Martin, and Stewart. It was soon revealed we were to "cut a conspicuous figure" in a war dance. We have among us frequent ideal representations of savage customs which are horrible enough, but the mind labors and struggles in vain to select from the wide range of our language the exact words that will properly describe an Indian war dance round a real captive. They came forth bedizened in their traps and feathers, their tomahawks and scalping knives in their uplifted hands, great daubs of red paint above and below their eyes, circling round and round us on a spasmodic trot, uttering their hoarse guttural songs, which seemed to flow up through their savage throats over sharp rifts of phlegm. As they proceeded, their pace, such as it was, accelerated, and their songs grew loud and louder, rising gradually from a monotonous grunt into a hideous and indescribable howl. Very often, some one of them, deserting his place, would dart towards us with his drawn hatchet threatening to brain us, while another would seize us by the hair and go through the pantomime of scalping. Thus, for two hours, they continued to sing and dance, and whoop and yell, flourishing their tomahawks and knives over us, until, at last they were compelled to stop from mere exhaustion. The captives were then separated, myself being led back to the chief's tent, where I was tied down to stakes in the manner before described. Four days had now passed without repose, but weary nature, at length, demanded rest, and I sank into a troubled sleep.

CHAPTER 11

In the morning I was released from the uncomfortable position I had occupied during the night, allowed to sit up with only my hands tied behind my back, a change which afforded inexpressible relief. I soon comprehended the number and character of the household in which necessity had forced me to take up board and lodging for an indefinite period of time. It consisted of a tall, stout Indian, who had apparently long passed the middle age of life, and his four wives. The latter were comparatively young, none of them exceeding twenty-three or twenty-four years. The youngest was by far the most comely and graceful and evidently the favorite. Each wife, as is the Comanche custom, had her separate and distinct apartment, consisting of a small tent erected outside of, but adjoining, the husband's.

Modern improvements have not been carried so far among them as to furnish the convenience of bells, such as are used to call waiters in our fashionable hotels, but as a substitute mine host of the wigwam had tied a deerskin cord to the corner of each of his wives's buffalo mattresses, the other end extending under the canvas into his own tent, thus rendering only a slight twitch necessary to communicate intelligence their presence was required. It was their duty to attend him, come at his call and go at his bidding, standing towards him as much in the relation of slaves as of wives.

He was the civil chief as distinguished from the war chief, and consequently the head of the tribe. This dignity carried with it the privilege of possessing four wives, a common Indian being allowed to have but one, subordinate officers two, and the war chief three. His name was Osolo, which, translated into Anglo Saxon, signifies "the Big Wolf." He had eight children, four of whom still remained in their mothers' tents, two had grown to manhood and taken wives to themselves, while two daughters had likewise left the paternal wigwam for the matrimonial lodge.

I had an opportunity now of observing their manner of preparing and partaking breakfast, which certainly was not attended with an extraordinary ceremony or display. Outside the tent, in front of the door, two logs lay side by side. Between them the fire was kindled. A long slice of horseflesh was attached to the end of a stick, some four feet in length, by which the meat was held over the fire, and when barely warmed through was brought into the tent, the handle end of the stick thrust into the ground, the long slice dangling from the other end, resembling a drooping blood-red flag. Kiln-dried corn was next boiled and mashed and served in a large dish made of bark. Breakfast was then ready, when, without more ado, each cut off a piece of meat, the size regulated by their appetites, and holding it between the fingers of one hand, with the fingers of the other scooped up the corn, filling their mouths alternately with flesh and vegetable.

An hour or two subsequently, a party of fifty, perhaps, collected together and held a council, the Big Wolf presiding. It was evident that frequent references were made to me, and that I was spoken of in connection with the watch. In the course of the consultation, Moko, the chief's favorite wife, into whose sacred keeping it had been delivered, was called. Presenting it to me, she made the usual signs, signifying, "Make it go." On this occasion I resolved to risk, for the first time, the result of a refusal. Accordingly I pointed to the heavens, uttering a rigmarole of words without sense or connection, and solemnly shook my head. If I did not impress them with the fact that such an operation, just at that time, would be attended with "the wreck of matter and the crush of worlds," it was not because of any lack of effort on my part. My success far exceeded my expectations. Instead of exhibiting any manifestations of ill humor, they quietly submitted to the disappointment, and continued their consultation.

Immediately after the council had adjourned, I discovered the warriors assembling outside the village at a point distant a quarter of a mile. I was somewhat curious to learn the occasion of it, but I little dreamed it was the prelude to an exhibition horrible beyond measure. At length, I was waited upon by a strong guard and escorted into their midst. On arriving, I found my fellow captives had preceded me, and at once comprehended some terrible scene would ensue. There were Aikens, Martin, and Stewart, stripped entirely naked, and bound as follows: Strong, high posts, had been driven in the ground about three feet apart. Standing between them, their arms had been drawn up as far as they could reach, the right hand tied to the stake on the right side and the left hand to the stake opposite. Their feet, likewise, were tied to the posts near the ground. Martin and Stewart were thus strung up side by side. Directly in front of them, and within ten feet, was Aikens, in the same situation. A short time sufficed to divest me of my scanty Indian apparel and place me by the side of the latter, and in like condition. Thus we stood, or rather hung. Aikens and myself facing Stewart and Martin, all awaiting in tormenting suspense to learn what diabolical rite was now to be performed.

The Big Wolf and a number of his old men stationed themselves near us, when the war chief, at the head of the warriors, of whom there were probably two hundred, moved forward slowly, silently, and in single file. Their pace was peculiar and difficult to describe, half walk, half shuffle, a spasmodic, nervous motion, like the artificial motion of figures in a puppet show. Each carried in one hand his knife or tomahawk, in the other a flint stone, three inches or more in length and fashioned into the shape of a sharp pointed arrow. The head of the procession as it circled a long way round, first approached Stewart and Martin. As it passed them, two of the youngest warriors broke from the line, seized them by the hair, and scalped them, then resumed their places and moved on. This operation consists of cutting off only a portion of the skin which covers the skull, of the dimensions of a dollar, and does not necessarily destroy life, as is very generally supposed; on the contrary, I have seen men, resident on the borders of Texas, who had been scalped and yet were alive and well. In this instance, the wounds inflicted were by no means mortal; nevertheless, blood flowed from them in profusion, running down over the face, and trickling from their long beards.

They passed Aikens and myself without molestation, marching round again in the same order as before. Up to this time there had been entire silence, except a yell from the two young men when in the act of scalping, but now the whole party halted a half-minute, and slapping their hands upon their mouths, united in a general and energetic war whoop. Then in silence the circuitous march was continued. When they reached Stewart and Martin the second time, the sharp flint arrowheads were brought into requisition. Each man, as he passed, with a wild screech, would brandish his tomahawk in their faces an instant, and then draw the sharp point of the stone across their bodies, not cutting deep, but penetrating the flesh just far enough to cause the blood to ooze out in great crimson gouts. By the time the line had passed, our poor suffering companions presented an awful spectacle. Still they left Aikens and myself as yet unharmed; nevertheless, we regarded it as a matter of certainty that very soon we should be subjected to similar tortures. We would have been devoutly thankful at that terrible hour—would have hailed it as a grateful privilege—could we have been permitted to choose our own mode of being put to death. How many times they circled round, halting to sound the war whoop, and going through the same demoniac exercise, I cannot tell. Suffice it to say, they persisted in the hellish work until every inch of the bodies of the unhappy men was haggled, and hacked and scarified, and covered with clotted blood. It would have been a relief to me, much more to them, could they have only died, but the object of the tormentors was to drain the fountain of their lives by slow degrees.

In the progress of their torture, there occurred an intermission of some quarter of an hour. During this period, some threw themselves on the ground and lighted their pipes, others collected in little groups, all, however, laughing and shouting, and pointing their fingers at the prisoners in derision, as if taunting them as cowards and miscreants. The prisoners bore themselves differently. Stewart uttered not a word, but his sobs and groans were such as only the intensest pain and agony can wring from the human heart. On the contrary, the pitiful cries and prayers of Martin were unceasing. Constantly he was exclaiming—"Oh! God have mercy on me!" "Oh, Father in heaven pity me!" "Oh! Lord Jesus, come and put me out of pain!" and many other expressions of like character.

I hung down my head and closed my eyes to shut out from sight the heart-sickening scene before me, but this poor comfort was not vouchsafed me. They would grasp myself, as well as Aikens, by the hair, drawing our heads back violently, compelling us, however unwillingly, to stare directly at the agonized and writhing sufferers.

At the end of, perhaps, two hours came the last act of the fearful tragedy. The warriors halted on their last round in the form of a half-circle, when two of them moved out from the center, striking into the war dance, raising the war song, advancing, receding, now moving to the right, now to the left, occupying ten minutes in proceeding as many paces. Finally, they reached the victims, for some time danced before them, as it were, the hideous dance of hell, then drew their hatchets suddenly, and sent the bright blades crashing through their skulls.

The bodies were taken down and rudely thrown aside upon the ground. What mattered it? They were at rest at last.

Aikens and myself now anticipated we would be compelled to suffer the same fate, and endeavored to prepare ourselves to meet it. To our astonishment, however, we were unbound, taken in charge by separate guards, reinvested in our hunting shirts and leggins, and started towards the camp. As we moved off, I turned my head to take a last lingering look at my dead companions, and saw that the Indian dogs had already gathered round the corpses and were lapping the blood from their innumerable wounds.

Returned to the same tent from which I had been taken to witness these barbarities, and again tied hand and foot, it may well be imagined I had abundant food for reflection. My contemplations were disheartening, indeed. Fully impressed with the belief that the novelty of the watch would presently pass away, and that it was foreordained, sooner or later, I must also suffer in like manner at the stake, the prevailing thought with me was how I might reach death, yet avoid their tortures. Self-destruction became a subject upon which I meditated, long and seriously. It was, however, a subject most repugnant to my nature. Whether, at any time, I would have taken my own life, if the means to do it had been allowed me, I can hardly determine; as it was, every instrument necessary to effect such a purpose was kept wholly beyond my reach.

The more I mused on the atrocities I had seen—the more the bleeding, ghastly forms of Stewart and Martin rose before me, as they did constantly day and night, both in my waking and sleeping hours—the more bitter became my feelings towards their murderers. My bosom scorched and burned with the desire of vengeance. I luxuriated in daydreams—became lost in the labyrinth of imagination—at one time fancying myself with an invading army come to sweep the barbarisms from the face of the earth—at another with my old companions in arms, the Texas Rangers, dashing upon them, slaughtering and slaying until they whined for mercy, like their own vile curs.

Indulging such moods as these, I was one day unbound and ordered to perform some menial office. Previously, however, I had determined in my heart to kill at least one or more of them the first opportunity that offered, partly to gratify my vengeance, but more especially actuated by the hope that in the melee, prompted by sudden wrath, they would dispatch me at once and save me from a lingering death at the stake. When, therefore, the cords were unfastened and I stood erect with free limbs, instead of obeying the command, I seized the first thing within my reach, which happened to be a wooden pothook, and hurled it at an Indian with all my strength. Well was it for him that it missed its aim. Instantly I was surrounded and borne down, but instead of producing the effect intended, the unexpected assault convulsed them with laughter. The next day, and the next, and every few days thereafter, I was unloosed and directed to skin a deer, or bring wood or water, they taking special care, in the meantime, to keep all dangerous weapons out of my reach and a sufficient number about me to prevent serious mischief. But I refused, absolutely and defiantly. On occasions, also, at this period, when the watch was brought out, I would not touch it. The life I was leading had become so inconceivably irksome—they were such a filthy and cruel race—the disgusting camp so "smelled to heaven"— everything about me was so hopeless and so wretched that I became utterly reckless, longing only to shake off, I cared not how, at length, the heavy nightmare of existence. If, therefore, I had previously feigned the character of a humble and devout missionary with some degree of success, I now played the part of an obstinate jackass to absolute perfection.

I had not seen Aikens since the day we separated at "the place of torment." What fate had befallen him was altogether unknown to me. It was, consequently, with much surprise that I saw him one day led into my tent, surrounded by a formidable guard. He was permitted to sit down beside me and an hour's time was granted, during which we were at liberty to converse.

He was far more familiar with Indian life and customs than myself, understood their signs and language better, so much more that I placed great reliance on his judgment. From him I learned that he had been kept a close prisoner in a tent on the outskirts of the village, and had experienced severer treatment than I had been subjected to—that he was now about to be carried to some distant tribe, and that this interview was allowed in order that we might have an opportunity of bidding each other farewell. No man could foresee his destiny, he said, but as for his own, there remained not a lingering doubt in his mind but that he was doomed to die by torture. He accounted for not having suffered with Stewart and Martin by saying it was not their custom to put more than two to death, in that way, at the same time; but he was convinced it was their intention to sacrifice him as soon as the tribe was reached they were now about to visit. However, not the shadow of an opportunity to escape should be lost, even though the chances against him were as ten thousand to one.

This was his judgment as regarded himself, but as to me, he was confident that with proper caution and prudence, I might eventually, through the instrumentality of the watch, be enabled to escape. He had witnessed the effect it had produced on the chiefs and warriors assembled in the square on our first arrival; and his knowledge of Indian ignorance and superstition was sufficient to teach him that they believed, in truth, it was a living spirit in a silver body.

When I recounted all that had occurred since we last separated—my refusal to wind it— my obstinacy in resisting their commands, and my attack upon the Indian when unbound, he became still more convinced. The fact they had pursued such a course towards me, which they had not towards him, was perfect evidence in his mind they intended to naturalize me, and that, so long, at least, as the watch remained in order, I need not fear death at their hands. But he advised me, by all means, to pursue an entirely different course from that lately adopted; on the contrary, to leave no effort untried to initiate myself into their favor—to cultivate their good will—to yield submission in all things, and to deceive them, if possible, into the belief that I preferred to dwell with them rather than with my own people. By pursuing this course, he represented the time would come at last when their vigilance would relax, and an opportunity of escaping safely from them would occur. We conversed of many things, past, present, and to come, losing not a moment of the precious hour. At its close, he was ordered by the guard to leave. Charging me, if ever I escaped, to communicate the intelligence of his misfortunes to his friend, Antonio Ferandez, of Corpus Christi, he bade me a sorrowful adieu, and passed out of the tent. I have never seen or heard of him since.

Soon after this, early one morning, I discovered the squaws busily engaged taking down the tents. One after another the dingy white cones came down until the whole village looked as if some sudden tempest had laid it in ruins. Every canvas, buffalo mattress, and blanket was then rolled up, the cooking kettles and the tent poles collected, and all packed firmly on the backs of a crowd of mules collected in the square. It was a busy and laborious scene, requiring much strength to elevate some of the packages to their place, yet it was all performed by women.

The Comanche Indian in his village is the idlest, laziest being in existence, a sluggard and a glutton. His sole and only pursuits are war and hunting. His wife, besides attending to the domestic duties of the tent, plants his corn and reaps it, cultivates his tobacco, tans his buffalo hides— in fine, performs wholly, without the remotest aid from him, every particle and kind of labor, which, among civilized beings, devolves upon the husband. So now, while the women toiled and strained and lifted, the men moped stupidly around, smoking their pipes, or lolled upon the ground.

Everything in readiness, I was once more blindfolded, mounted, and tied, when the entire town, not only its men, women, and children, but its furniture, its tents, its public and private buildings, all moved off on the backs of mules and horses. There was not left one stone upon another of that city.

Fortunately, the mule upon which I rode was led, so that I escaped the annoyance that befell me, under similar circumstances, on a previous occasion: Being deprived of the use of my eyes on the journey, except when we encamped at night, I cannot give a description of the country over which we passed, further than to say we crossed over many mountains, and that it seemed to me a wild and barren region. At the end of three days, or three "sleeps," as a Comanche would express it, we reached the end of the journey. Here I found myself in a small village, of not more than twenty or thirty tents, inhabited by what appeared to be a portion of Big Wolf's tribe, on the bank of a considerable river that flowed to the southwest, and in a valley much larger than any I have before described.

CHAPTER 12

On our arrival, which was welcomed with no demonstrations whatever, the squaws unpacked the mules, and immediately engaged in erecting the tents, with the same assiduity they exhibited in taking them down. In a few days, though an hundred miles distant, we were, to all appearances, occupying the same village, having the same square, and the same streets—which in fact we were, save that it was located on a different spot, and contained a population numbering about two hundred more.

The valley, also, was a "counterfeit presentment" of the one we had left behind, except the stream whereon we had encamped was wider, and the mountains round about seemed to have fallen back. It was called Mannasaw, laying a heavy accent on the last syllable, the meaning whereof I do not know.

In time I came to understand that this was the usual summer residence of the tribe, where their corn and beans and tobacco were cultivated—that it, in fact, was their main camping ground, their home, and that the other valley was only resorted to for the purpose of hunting, during those moons when the hair on the buffalo is thick and long. In the suburbs of this village were extensive specimens of Indian agriculture. The Comanche women— for the men have nothing whatever to do with it—would not be likely to receive even a "volume of the Transactions," were they to compete for the prize offered for the best system of farming at one of our state fairs. The expense of drainage and subsoil ploughing is small; nevertheless, they manage to raise respectable crops.

The confidence I had in the shrewdness and judgment of Aikens, and the encouragement I had received from him in our interview, inspired me with hope, and I resolved to follow his advice to the letter. My fame, evidently, had spread abroad through the new community soon after our arrival, for those I had never seen before came and gazed upon me for a long time, and then turned and walked seriously and thoughtfully away. It was not long before Moko came with a group of the new faces and presented me the watch. My obstinacy was now abandoned, and I fell again, very deep, into the mysterious mood. Winding it up and setting the alarm a minute or two ahead, I bowed my face before it—clasped it affectionately to my bosom—

held it out at arm's length before me in my two hands, regarding it with that intensity of expression with which a tragedian on the stage always regards a love letter just received—turning up my eyes adoringly towards the glorious heavens—and let it whiz!

The effect was solemn and satisfactory. I felt that I had made "a hit"— that the sharp eyes which could detect a trail so far had failed to penetrate the thin veil which covered the deception. Up to this time, and never afterwards, did they attempt to open it, or exhibit any inclination to manage it themselves; nor did any other than Moko, the youngest wife of Big Wolf, ever have it in charge.

Moreover, I now became submissive, and when untied obeyed every order that was given me. I ran to the waterside and filled the Big Wolf's buffalo horn when he was thirsty, pounded his corn when he was hungry, spread his mattress and lighted his pipe, in fine, made myself generally useful. As Aikens had predicted, their vigilance did relax to such a degree that I was permitted to wander through the village, but not beyond it—to have a knife in my possession—to sleep without being bound—and so far ingratiated myself into their confidence and esteem that they christened me Chemahacho—"the good white man."

This was not done, however, until after I had entered into a solemn league and covenant with the chief. It was a singular bond, not to be found in any book or legal forms. A stick of wood eight or ten inches long and about two inches square was produced. On its different sides were carved numerous figures representing skeletons, scalps, tomahawks and other like devices. Receiving the stick from Big Wolf, I opened a vein on the back of my hand and carefully painted the carved characters with blood. The condition of this sanguinary agreement, as it was understood, at least by the party of one part, was that I would remain in the quiet and peaceable possession of said Big Wolf, his heirs and assigns, without any attempt, design, effort, idea, or intention of running away, while he, the aforesaid Big Wolf, on his part, for and in consideration thereof, covenanted, promised, bargained, agreed, and solemnly obligated himself, in case I did, to make a skeleton of me in the shortest possible space of time, according to the Indian statutes in such case made and provided.

Though closely observed, and confined within certain limits, like one out on bail in the old times of imprisonment for debt, I now enjoyed comparative freedom; and as day after day and week after week passed wearily away, had opportunities of observing their habits, customs, and peculiarities, and to become thoroughly conversant with life in a Comanche camp.

As before stated, the sole business of the male portion of the tribe was war and hunting. While in camp the Indian is idle, listless, sleeping the greater part of the day and all night. He is slovenly in his dress, except when he meets in council or goes on the warpath, when he decorates himself with the scalps he has taken, which at other times hang in his tent. His prowess as a warrior is estimated in proportion to the number he possesses.

The most renowned brave in the camp of the Big Wolf—he who could boast the possession of the greatest number of these trophies—was Hawakakeno, the Wide River. He was, indeed, a brawny and powerful savage, terrible in battle and quarrelsome in the village. He was feared as well as admired; his word was law among his weaker brethren, and none of all his tribe could stand before him in single contest.

To supply the necessaries of life, more or less are constrained daily to go out upon the hunt. In this, their only labor, they range within a circuit rarely extending more than four or five miles from the town. Their weapons, on these excursions, are the bow and arrow and the lance, both of which they use with great dexterity and skill, especially on horseback. Indeed, in the matter of horsemanship, I doubt whether there is a race on the face of the whole earth that equals the Comanches. They will lie along the sides of their horses, while under full speed, directing their course at the same time and discharging arrows from under their necks with deadly effect, in a manner astonishing to witness.

If a deer is captured, he brings it in on his horse, throws it to the women whose business is to dress and cook it. If he kills a mustang or a buffalo, he rides into the village and informs his squaw where the carcass may be found, who straightway mounts and goes out in search of it— skins it — cuts the flesh into strips, and returns.

While the men are thus indolent, the women are remarkable for their industry. Besides attending to the menial duties of the camp, working in the fields during the planting and harvesting seasons, they perform extraordinary labors in preparing buffalo hides and bringing them into the soft and pliant condition in which we see them. To do this properly requires about six weeks, and the process may be new to many of my readers.

When the hide is first brought in green, it is placed upon a log so hewed that it presents a flat surface, perhaps a foot in width. With an instrument similar to a common adze, the squaws cut away all the flesh and part of the bulkiest portions of the hide, until the whole presents a uniform thickness. This is a long and tedious operation. They are then stretched upon frames, and rubbed with a kind of pumice stone until the surface becomes furzy. If it should dry in this state, however, it would be hard, stiff and unpliant. To avoid this, they use a preparation composed of basswood bark pounded very fine and mixed with the brains of the deer or buffalo, which is applied day after day until the skin is thoroughly saturated, when it is soft and flexible.

The buffalo robe is the principal, and indeed, so far as I know, their only article of commerce—their only source of wealth. At a certain season every year they are transported to the confines of Mexico, and sold to parties of Mexican traders who annually meet them there, and receive in compensation hatchets, knives, and such other implements as are used by them, together with cheap calicoes, mescal, and a great variety of trinkets.

It has previously been stated that the men dress in buckskin. The women do likewise, to a great extent, but most of them wear a sort of short gown made of the calico thus obtained. Children, until they arrive at the age of eight or nine, do not take the trouble to dress in anything.

In their personal habits they are supremely nasty. Occasionally, in warm weather, they bathe in the river, but daily ablutions are not thought of, so that they are constantly covered with dirt and vermin.

The institution of marriage is recognized, and governed by established laws. When a young man becomes enamored and resolves to take a wife, he presents himself before the council and makes known his desire. If there are no objections on the part of the maiden or her parents, the council decrees that they may live together in the matrimonial relation one moon. If, at the end of that time, there has arisen no dissension between them, and they are mutually satisfied, they are permitted to continue the relation another moon, and if they live together harmoniously through that, the knot is irrevocably tied. The system of matrimony among them, therefore, seems to be founded on the principle of the rule of three.

Equally peculiar is their mode of burial. When a warrior dies, his body is carried out and laid upon the ground, his head always toward the west. A pen is then built up around him constructed of poles. Into this enclosure is placed his personal effects—his saddle and bridle, his tomahawk, scalping knife, bow and arrows and lance, all the inanimate property he possesses. The enclosure is then roofed with bark and covered with earth. This part of the burial ceremony concluded, all his horses and mules, even if he was the owner of a hundred, are brought to the grave and killed. When a squaw dies, her property, also—her calico gown, cooking kettle, tools for dressing skins—are buried with her, and the horse upon which she was accustomed to ride slain in the same manner.

They are buried with their heads to the west, because they believe at the resurrection, of which they have vague and indefinite notions, they will arise and march eastward, again to take possession of all the country from which the accursed white man has driven them and their fathers. They bury their property with them and kill their horses because they suppose their souls will have need of them in the other world.

Among them are prophets, corresponding with our divines, who maintain with exceeding strictness their sacerdotal dignity. The prophet addresses them on various occasions, such as the green corn dance, and the festival of the roasted dog, but especially in the time of the new moon. At all times they listen to him with the most profound reverence, their heads hanging down, and not a murmur of sound among them from the commencement of his exhortation to its close; but in the season of the new moon, they fall on their faces to the earth before him, and there remain still and motionless until the sound of his voice has ceased.

They believe in God, a great spirit, who created and governs the earth, sun, moon, and stars. They have an unwavering and undoubting faith in a future state of existence, and in future rewards and punishments. They hold that the soul of the wicked coward or thief, after death, will be driven before the frown of the Great Spirit, afar off into a region barren and cold and desolate, there to wander forever through thorns and among rocks, thirsty, hungry, and in pain; but the good Indian, who has been brave in battle and walked uprightly among his tribe, will be translated to a valley ten thousand times ten thousand fold longer and wider than their own valley of Mannasaw, where the climate is always mild as it is in the moon of plants; where there is cool water, and pounded corn and mustang meat forever at his hand, and where buffalo and deer abound, and the horses are fleeter than the wind.

They have many traditions but no records; nevertheless, they have certain hieroglyphics by which they contrive to communicate intelligence with as much accuracy as if they understood the epistolary art. For instance, if one party goes out before another has returned, and wishes to convey information of the course they have taken and the business they are upon, they will seek some point where it is probable their trail will be discovered. Here, providing themselves with a thin piece of birch bark, which can be folded in the form of a letter without breaking, they will make such figures and emblems upon it as represent the idea they wish to convey. If they are on the war path, the character will be a tomahawk and a scalp; if on a visit to a friendly tribe, it will be a pipe; if on a buffalo or deer hunt, there will be no characters, but the folded bark will simply enclose some of the hair of the animal of which they are in pursuit. If they intend to be absent a month, the emblem will be the full moon; if two weeks, a half-moon, if only a few days, the new moon. Then they strike a hatchet deep into the trunk of a tree, and withdrawing it, place the end of the bark epistle in the incision, the outer end pointing in the direction they have taken. It will be seen they measure time by the changes of the moon. In the new, they give themselves up to devotional contemplation and worship, rendering thanks unto the Great Spirit that although the old one has gone, another has been permitted to take its place. Every change is attended with some peculiar ceremony; but when it is in the full, occurs the festival of the roasted dog. With the exception of the refreshments, it differs but very slightly from a modern picnic. The squaws go out to a spring in some pleasant and shady spot, taking with them a number of curs, which have been fattened for the occasion, and kindling a fire, butcher and roast them. By this time the warriors approach, when, seating themselves promiscuously on the grass, they speedily strip the canine bones admidst much fun and laughter. On these occasions, while I was with them, Sahonkeno, the Fox— a lively and mischievous rascal—was always the life of the party.

Not long after my arrival in the valley of Mannasaw, took place the first exhibition I had witnessed of the green corn dance. This occurs in the latter part of July, or the hot moon. The day previous to the festival, a general meeting of the whole tribe was held in the square of the village. In the center stood the prophet, Karolo, signifying, as near as I was ever able to comprehend, a star, or planet; immediately around him, in a circle, were gathered the chiefs and principal men, seated on the ground; behind these were the warriors, and in the rear the women and children.

Karolo, the prophet, addressed them long and earnestly, and made many gestures. Though I could not understand his language, I knew from his manner and the intonations of his voice that the sentiments to which he gave expression came from the inmost depth of his heart. So near as I was able to comprehend, he was commenting on the wonderful goodness of the Great Spirit who gave them green corn in its season, and exhorting them to thankfulness for the same.

The next day, outside the village, numerous fires were kindled at short distances from each other round a large circle, which included between one and two acres. Each family had its separate fire, and by each fire was a quantity of green corn, piled on a buffalo skin. When the squaws had roasted it, the prophet, the civil and war chiefs, and a few others took a position in the center of the circle, while the tribe, numbering some six hundred, ranged themselves outside the fires, and the dance began. Round and round they went, singing their green corn song, which sounded in my ears like the perpetual repetition of "ahow, aho, aho, ahow," keeping time to rude specimens of music hammered out of a dry skin drawn over a hoop, and extracted from a quick and violent collision of buffalo bones—a performance similar to that common among Negro minstrels. Finally, they huddled together on the south side of the circle, and sat down. Karolo addressed them briefly, and was followed in a few remarks by the chiefs. The prophet then walked around the circle, raising his hands above the separate piles of roasted corn as he passed them, talking all the while, as if invoking a blessing, and having made the circuit, the tribe gathered in distinct squads about the several fires and commenced eating. When the roasted ears were shelled to the last kernel, the festival of the green corn dance was over, and they went back, singing, to the town.

It is a custom among them to paint their faces daily. I was compelled, every morning, while with them, to pursue this practice—to anoint my features with a preparation composed chiefly of a peculiar kind of clay—so that it would be difficult for a stranger to distinguish me from one of their own number. As I became more and more acquainted with those who inhabited the little village we had joined, I observed four girls, the youngest twelve, and the oldest, perhaps, eighteen, whose appearance attracted my attention. They had the copper-colored complexion, but not the high cheekbones and the course black hair and the peculiar expression of countenance that always distinguish the aborigines. On the other hand, they possessed the Anglo-Saxon face—their gait was different from that of the other women of the tribe—and what was the most extraordinary, they had fine light hair, inclined to auburn, and upon one of them it curled. They were a mystery to me, until one day I saw the women coming from the river where they had gone to bathe, and walking among them were these four, perfectly white. The paint had been washed from their faces in the water, revealing to me their race. I made assiduous inquiries of Big Wolf and others, and of themselves, but could obtain no satisfactory information. They knew no other than the language of the Comanches, and in all respects conformed to their manners and customs. It was, therefore, evident to me they had been captured in early childhood and remembered no other life than that they were then leading.

More or less of the tribe were almost constantly absent on the warpath. Sometimes they would sally forth of their own motion; at others, a number of them would join a party from a different village happening to pass that way. Eventually they returned, and the manner of their approach indicated whether they had been successful, or the reverse. On one occasion, during the summer, they brought in a captive, blindfolded as I had been, and had a rousing war dance over him in the square. I longed for the privilege of speaking to him, but it was denied. The morning following his advent, he was tied on a mule, his face covered with buckskin, and escorted from the camp. I never could gain the least information from whence he came, or whither he was taken; but suppose he had been captured by a party belonging to another village, who simply halted at our encampment overnight, and got up the war dance by way of entertainment.

We were frequently visited by the chiefs and warriors of the surrounding tribes. They were, invariably, cordially welcomed and hospitably entertained. Then there was a pipe dance, which is the dance of love and friendship. They were invited to repose on the largest buffalo skins, and given to eat the flesh of a roasted dog, though the moon was not in the full—a luxury surpassing even the meat of the wild horse. I apprehend many were attracted to our camp through curiosity to see and hear the wonderful watch, the fame thereof, beyond question, having spread far and near. I come to this conclusion from the fact that speedily following their arrival, Moko would bring it forth, and call on me to make it talk.

There was one visitor, in particular, a stout, surly chief, who in the course of the summer visited our camp many times. He appeared to have become fascinated with the watch, never growing weary of listening to the alarm. After Moko had finally placed it affectionately in her bosom, he would have long and earnest interviews with Big Wolf, the subject of their conversation being, as was easy to perceive, the mysterious watch. I learned that he was the chief of a tribe whose village was situated in a valley beyond the mountains at the distance of two days' journey, and that he was known as the Spotted Leopard.

Lounging about the camp, I now led a monotonous and weary life until about November, or, at least, until after the season of buffalo hunting had arrived, when I was ordered, unexpectedly, one morning, to mount a mule, and riding forth from the camp, accompanied by Big Wolf and half a dozen of his warriors, I left behind me forever the beautiful valley of Mannasaw.

CHAPTER 13

On this journey I was neither tied or blindfolded, but rode a bridled mule, while the warriors were mounted on their best horses. They usually kept me in advance of them, directing me when to turn to the right and left. We followed a well-beaten trail that led in a northwest direction. On reaching the head of the valley, we turned to the left, and began the ascent of a wide, low range of mountains, winding in and out of narrow passes and defiles, but still gradually ascending, traveling in this manner some twenty miles before reaching the summit. The descent on the opposite side was of equal extent.

The ravines were overgrown with dwarfish trees, and the adjacent mountains in general were rocky, but occasionally between the ridges that rose in succession one above the other were small, level plats, covered with a heavy growth of grass, upon which buffalo, deer, and antelopes were feeding.

While crossing one of these little prairies, we espied a bear making his way to the mountain. A part of the Indian's equipage is a lasso, tied to his saddle girth, and in the skill and accuracy with which they throw it, they far excel the Mexicans. On this occasion it was brought into use. A couple of them galloped out, one dexterously throwing the noose over Bruin's neck and twitching him on his back, the other as dexterously throwing another over his hind legs, thus subjecting him to a most uncomfortable stretch, as they pulled in opposite directions. A scalping knife soon relieved him of his hide, and a portion of his carcass supplied our evening meal. Bear's flesh is often eaten by them, but is not regarded as equal to buffalo, beef, or venison. They are hunted considerably, however, for their oil, which is used in the preparation of various kinds of skins.

Having descended the western slope of the mountain range, we encamped that night at the extreme point of a narrow valley, which seemed to run up a long distance between the hills. Wearied with a hard day's travel, I hastened to cook my own and Big Wolf's supper—for I was compelled to act towards him in the capacity of a servant—and then lay down to rest. Though I brought his water, and cooked his food, and slept in his tent, and was in fact, his menial and slave, Big Wolf never, in a single instance, placed the horn of water to his lips or put a morsel of flesh into his mouth until I had tasted them. This, also, was the case with the two chiefs to whom I subsequently belonged. Whether it was through fear of poison, or dictated by some singular superstition, is more than I am able to determine.

Setting out again early in the morning, we traveled down the little winding valley until it opened into an extensive plain. Here we struck a narrow but very rapid stream, when turning to the right, round the point of a high bluff we rode along its banks, discovering as we advanced broken patches of prairie where it was evident some tribe had grown its last year's corn. The valley is called, in the Indian tongue, Lescoha, and the stream, which we were following towards its source, Boge Lescoha.

In the afternoon we came in sight of a large town situated directly at the foot of a mountain which bounded the plain on its northern side. A mile outside we were met by a party of eight or ten, who approached us on a dashing gallop and escorted us in. When we had reached the square, the same surly chief who had so often visited Big Wolf to listen to the voice of that wonderful thing which Moko carried in her bosom came forward and bade us welcome. Then I knew we were in the camp of the Spotted Leopard.

The village was built on both sides of the Boge Lescoha, which had its source in a large spring under the mountain, not far distant. It divided the town in the center, the civil chief's tent being on one side and the war chief's on the other.

A short half-hour only had passed, when the horn sounded the war dance. I was conducted to the center somewhat nervous and apprehensive—the apparitions of Martin and Stewart flitting before my mental vision—nevertheless, there remained an inward confidence I would not be put to death, because I had kept the covenant. While in this state of perplexity, the warriors were issuing from their tents, whither they had gone when the horn sounded, to gird on their belts, and decorate themselves with such scalps as they possessed, and were assembling round me. The signal given, the dance began, and was conducted in the usual manner, such as I have before attempted to describe, but which the reader must see before he can fully understand. It was brief—unusually so—and terminated without any damage, very much to my relief.

After the ceremony, I was conducted to the tent of one of the Spotted Leopard's wives, of whom he also had four. This was especially appropriated to the accommodation of Big Wolf, and inasmuch as I had always slept in the same tent with him at home, he did not think proper to alter the programme on this occasion.

In the morning, a large number of mules and horses were collected in the square, driven in from the surrounding pasture by the women. Piles of buffalo, deer, and beaver skins, also, were brought from the tents and packed on mules. I was then brought out by Big Wolf, who produced the bloody stick and delivered it to the Spotted Leopard, at the same time informing me I had been sold and assigned. To render the transfer legal, however, it became incumbent on me to reopen the vein on the back of my hand, and again stain the carved figures with blood, an act which, in view of the alternative of being butchered, I performed with great alacrity. This formality closed the bargain, when Big Wolf and his warriors departed, taking with them the avails of the sale. In this business transaction, I had the satisfaction of learning how much, in Indian estimation, I was worth, to wit: 120 animals, old and young, of the horse kind, and as many skins as three pack mules could carry.

From the first I entertained an inveterate dislike of the Spotted Leopard. He was morose, reserved, unsocial, and there was a malignant expression about his mouth and eyes that told me as plainly as if it had been written in emphatic English on his forehead that he was a being who would delight in cruelty. These were my first impressions of him, and I never had occasion to modify them afterwards. But among his wives, there was one who treated me with all the kindness I had previously received at the hands of Moko, the young consort of the Big Wolf, and she was Kianceta, the Weasel.

At the end of four days, Big Wolf again made his appearance, attended by his four wives and a number of warriors. Their arrival was celebrated by a pipe dance. This ceremony was conducted as follows: The wives of the two chiefs, myself, and several old men of the tribe were stationed in the center of the ring. At its side stood the Spotted Leopard, with a lighted pipe made of red sandstone. As the warriors danced around, each, as he came opposite the chief, received the pipe at his hands, took a whiff or two, and handed it back. This ceremony was accompanied by one of their wild and peculiar songs, and when it was concluded, Moko came forward with the watch, kissed it, presented it to me, and turning about, broke through the circle of warriors, crying, and disappeared in a neighboring tent.

I caused it to sound the alarm, probably a dozen times, when the Spotted Leopard approached me with Kianceta by his side. Into the possession of the latter, the weird, mysterious thing, through which the Great Spirit spoke in a strange voice, was delivered, and the crowd dispersed.

Kianceta, the Weasel, was tall and slim, and erect as the young cedar that grew on the bank of the Boge Lescoha. She had an easy and elastic gait, as if shod with velvet springs, and in her movements there was a nameless grace and dignity which drew all eyes after her, as the magnet attracts the steel. She was dressed in buckskin moccasins, and leggins colored red—a blue broadcloth skirt, tastefully embroidered with beads, and over this a bright calico short gown—articles obtained from the Mexican traders. Her long hair, blacker than the feathers of the crow, fell down over her shoulders in luxuriant profusion, halfway to the ground, and around her forehead was a tin band, scalloped on the upper edge, after the fashion of a crown.

Kianceta was indeed comely to look upon, but her soul was far more lovely than her form. Though an untutored woman of the prairie—one of a low and ignorant class—I have reason to remember her with respect and gratitude. She sympathized with the poor captive when others laughed at his calamities—sat down by his side, and looked up sorrowfully into his face, when the young savages in the village beat him with stones and sticks until he sought shelter in the tent. An hundred times she stood between him and those who threatened harm—gave him corn when others had it not— attended him when sick—casting red-hot stones into a trough of water to make him a steam bath, and wrapping him in thick buffalo skins until his cold was broken up and his health restored.

Next morning the tribe was assembled, and Che-ra-se-chick-a-lo, the prophet, made a speech. He was not as earnest and impressive as Karolo— palpably inferior in every respect— nevertheless, he was listened to with the most profound attention. At the conclusion of his exhortation, they indulged in a long and jolly feast, when Moko and the three other wives of Big Wolf came and kissed me again and again, and then bestriding their mules, rode away towards their own valley of Mannasaw, weeping as they went.

My time was now passed either in attending upon the Spotted Leopard, or sauntering idly through the village, continually thinking of escape. This subject was never out of my mind. By observing the rising and setting sun, I could tell the points of compass, and recalling, as far as possible, the direction of the different routes I had taken in my progress hither, made up my mind as to the course which would lead most directly to the white settlements. About half a mile from the camp was a deep, thickly timbered ravine, running back apparently a long distance among the mountains. I had been out to the entrance of this ravine with the chief in one of his rambles, and it occurred to me if I could manage to slip away from the camp unperceived, and get into it, escape was possible. Many a night my eyes were not closed in sleep, studying and musing over the plan. During the day I was constantly gazing toward the defile—some indefinable but powerful attraction turning my face thitherward.

Finally my plan was perfected—which was to steal away from the village in the night, trusting to travel many miles on the journey before the chief would awake. At length, after patient watching, the favorable moment, as I supposed, arrived. I was permitted at this time to carry a knife, and providing myself with some strips of venison, about twelve o'clock one night, when the chief was lost in deep slumber and the camp was silent, crawled softly from the tent and was about to make my way from the village and fly across the plain, when I was startled by the growl of a big dog, that confronted me, showing his white teeth. Presently he was joined by another, and another, until I found myself surrounded. Their growls awakened all the other curs, with which an Indian town is invariably overrun, and instantly a universal snarling and barking was heard from one end to the other of the camp. The disturbed women and warriors shouted to them, in a half-sleeping, half-waking state, to be still and lie down. Under these circumstances, further advance was useless, and I made my way back into the tent, as speedily and stealthily as the nature of my situation allowed, having in the meantime avoided observation.

Though disappointed beyond measure, I was by no means so far discouraged as to abandon the enterprise, but determined still more firmly to avail myself of the first opportunity that occurred to put it into execution.

My orders were not to go beyond the boundaries of the village. However, as their watchfulness over me became less and less strict, I so far disregarded them, occasionally, as to wander a short way down the creek, or out to a little grove some rods from the village—at times being told by anyone who chose to exercise the authority, to go back; at others, left to return at leisure. This practice I kept up, until finally it became almost unnoticed. Emboldened by their increasing indifference, just at dusk one evening, at that point of obscurity between light and darkness when objects may be seen at some distance on the plain, but when it is difficult to distinguish between a man and an animal, I started off at a slow, careless pace towards the mouth of the ravine. Having proceeded, perhaps, a hundred rods, and when about to make a trial of my speed, I saw three warriors in advance, approaching me directly. I happened, at this moment to be near a cluster of bushes, and taking out my knife commenced cutting a forked stick, designing to deceive them into the belief that my business there was to obtain such an article for the purpose of more conveniently cooking the Spotted Leopard's meat; but my movements, especially at that hour, were too suspicious, and they were, evidently, not to be deceived.

Taking me by the arm, they led me back into camp, and on arriving there, called the chief one side and had a lengthened interview with him. At its close the chief pointed me into his tent, where I was tied down to stakes, on my back, in the same manner I had been bound when first carried away into captivity. This, I supposed, was the extent of the penalty I was doomed to suffer, but a short time taught me I was sorely and painfully mistaken. The Spotted Leopard, drawing down my leggin, with the coolness of the most practiced surgeon, drew the edge of his knife across the cartilage or tendon just below the kneepan of my right leg. The muscle was not entirely severed, as was evidently his intention. The object of this surgical operation was to cripple me in such manner as to render escape impossible, even should a favorable opportunity present itself. For two weeks I was kept tied down, the chief frequently, during that time, bending the leg back and forth, each time breaking open the wound afresh. Eventually, however, I was unbound, and the wound permitted to heal, leaving a formidable cicatrice, and rendering the limb extremely stiff, not to such a degree, however, as it was his purpose to make it.

In the winter following, some 250 of the warriors, armed with bows and arrows, lances, tomahawks, and knives, set out on their annual grand buffalo hunt. They were mounted on their choice horses, while I, who accompanied the chief as his servant, rode, unarmed, a dilapidated mule.

It is only in the cold months that the skin of the buffalo has any value for the purposes of traffic. Then, only, is it covered with wool, being, in the warm summer weather, with the exception of a tuft of mane, entirely bare. During the latter period they are only killed as the necessity of food requires—their skins then being used for the construction of tents.

On these annual excursions, they are followed by a large number of mules that not only carry out their buffalo-hunting tents, which simply consist of one or more skins, thrown over a pole resting on crossed stakes—but also bring back the hides they may succeed in taking.

On the occasion I now refer to, the party moved west, threading their winding way over the mountains, and across numerous streams and valleys of greater or less width and extent. In the afternoon of the third day we struck a wide, rolling prairie. Dividing it nearly in the center was a high, smooth ridge—its summit reached from both sides by an easy, gradual ascent. As we crossed the prairie and approached this ridge, our scattered cavalcade extended, perhaps, a quarter of a mile, moving forward carelessly, and in no order whatever. I was at the extreme rear, by the side of the Spotted Leopard, and surrounded by the pack mules. As the foremost horsemen reached the height, they halted suddenly, making hurried signs, while two or three of the braves galloped back down the slope, riding eagerly to and fro among their brethren, as if urging them to push forward without delay. The whole band, thereupon, dashed up the hill, except the Spotted Leopard and myself, who remained with the mules in the rear, and on reaching the summit deployed into line. By this time I had heard the cry of "the Apaches, the Apaches," and knew at once there was hot work at hand.

As yet, however, I had seen nothing of an enemy, and only drew the inference there was one present from the cries I had heard, and the general commotion that prevailed. In the course of two or three minutes after our line formed on the ridge, the air was rent with the noise of the war whoop, and up the opposite ascent, at full speed, came the Apaches in solid body, like a black cloud. As they approached, a shower of arrows were discharged from both lines, when they rushed upon each other in a hand-to-hand encounter.

From the position I occupied I had a fair, unobstructed view of the battle. It was fierce and terrible. The horses reared, and plunged, and fell upon each other, their riders dealing blow for blow, and thrust for thrust, some falling from their saddles to the ground, and others trampling madly over them.

The Comanches outnumbered the enemy; nevertheless, they were forced to retreat, falling back down the hill almost to my position; but still they were not pursued, the Apaches appearing to be content to hold possession of the ground. Soon, the tribe of the Spotted Leopard again rallied and dashed once more to the attack. If possible, this contest was severer, as it was longer than the first. Again the fierce blow was given and returned; again horses and men intermingled in the melee—stumbled, fell, and rolled upon the ground, while the wide heavens resounded with their hideous shrieks and cries.

My blood thrilled through my veins as I looked upon the scene. I had mingled in encounters fierce even as that, but never before in the midst of the hottest fight was I overcome with such a sense of terror. To be an inactive spectator of a battle is far more painful than to be a participator in it.

I hoped devoutly during the engagement that the Comanches would be beaten, being impressed with the belief that if I should fall into the enemies' hands, my chances of escape would be increased, for I had often heard that the Apaches, though a most warlike nation, were more merciful to prisoners than others of their race. But in this I was disappointed. The Apaches at length gave way, disappearing beyond the ridge. Instead of pursuing their advantage, however, the Comanches hastily gathered up their dead and retreated towards the mountains we had crossed. As soon as they had left the ground, the Apaches again appeared upon the height, and bore away their dead also. It was a drawn battle.

This encounter was unexpected on both sides. The Apaches, as I learned, were gathered around a spring, cooking their meat, little expecting the approach of an enemy, when the van of our party came upon them. At that time a deadly strife existed between the tribes, and it would have been a scandalous violation of an Indian's idea of manhood to have separated, under such circumstances, without a bloody tilt at arms.

The Comanches lost in this battle seventeen warriors; the Apaches, probably as many more. Had the combatants belonged to a civilized people who keep a record of their wars, it would have furnished a thrilling page of history; but thousands of such sanguinary struggles take place on the lonely prairies of which the world knows not. That same season, however, they buried the tomahawk and danced the pipe dance, and henceforward were at peace.

The close of this eventful day was occupied in burying the slain, which ceremony was performed in their customary manner, except they seemed to chant the death song with more energy and feeling than on ordinary occasions. With them, death, at any time, even the nearest and dearest of their kindred, is not regarded as an event to be deplored, but on the contrary, to be welcomed with rejoicing; but when a warrior dies on the field of battle, their joy and exultation knows no bounds, for their crude theology assures them his departed spirit is, at once, caught up by the Great Spirit, and borne to the region of everlasting and supreme felicity.

We saw no more of the Apaches, and the following day turned our course up the prairie—crossed the mountains into a still wider prairie—and there, at a watering place, pitched our camp. Here we remained two months, meeting with unanticipated success. Thousands and thousands of buffalo, in immense droves, were roving over the plain, and it was an easy task to obtain as many hides as the mules could carry home.

On the return, which was by a different route from that we came, we fell in with a party of two or three hundred, a friendly tribe, who accompanied us back to the camp. Their chief was Kan-sa-le-um-ko, the Rolling Thunder. He was agreeable, though sedate—a compound of benign dignity and solemnity—a chief who plainly preferred falling on his face before the prophet, in the time of the new moon, to dancing the war dance with the warriors.

The Rolling Thunder and his tribe remained with us a week, and it was, indeed, a week of carnival and merriment. First of all was the war dance, and then followed the solemn discourses of Che-ra-se-chick-a-lo, the prophet, and after them came the ring dance and the pipe dance, and the feast of the roasted dog. During these entertainments, the good Kianceta and myself played a conspicuous part in the exhibition of the watch. As on all former occasions, it captivated the simple children of nature, and particularly the Rolling Thunder, whose reverent temperament led him to refer all mysteries, whether great or small, to the wonder-working power of the Great Spirit.

Soon after the departure of Rolling Thunder and his people came another large party and pitched their hunting tents on the bank of the stream, outside the town. The day following their arrival, I observed our warriors, belted, and decorated with trinkets and scalps, moving towards their encampment. Something unusual, I felt confident, was about to take place. Distant but a quarter of a mile, I could hear distinctly the sound of their voices singing their savage songs. Presently, came thrilling through the air, mingling with the loud, shrill war whoop, a shriek of mortal agony. Again and again it was repeated, growing fainter and fainter, until, finally, it ceased, or, at least, failed to reach my ears.

At length, a party of six or seven came after me. While passing through the strange encampment, I discovered pieces of soldier's clothing, which I recognized at once as the United States uniform. Moving on beyond the camp into a grove, a spectacle presented itself that froze my blood with horror. A white man had been subjected to the torture. He was not lashed to stakes as Stewart and Martin were, but a sharp stick had been thrust through his heel cords, by which he was suspended from a limb, with his head downward, as a butcher suspends a carcass in the shambles.

He, also, had been sacrificed with the accursed flints, his ears cut off, and tongue drawn out. A slight convulsive shrug of the shoulders indicated that life was not wholly extinct. I gazed upon him in silence and terror and was relieved when they led me away. I concluded, from what I saw in their camp, he was a United States soldier, captured, probably, near one of the frontier outposts—such exploits not being unusual, numbers having been taken during my early residence in Texas, as far down as Fort Jesup in Louisiana.

The Indian policy of the United States, I am convinced, is not the most advisable one. So long as it is continued, the frontier settlements will be constantly exposed to depredations, and prisoners subjected to the horrid cruelties I have described. They cherish an inveterate and undying hatred of the white race, whom they regard as usurpers and are sanguine in the belief that the time will eventually arrive when they will be enabled, with the assistance of the Great Spirit, to sweep them from existence and reclaim their rightful inheritance. In their ignorance, they compare, favorably for themselves, their feeble strength with the whole power of the United States.

It would be cheaper for the government, in the end, instead of maintaining a line of military posts on the frontier—standing merely on the defensive—to send an army through their territories, giving them ocular demonstrations of its power, arresting their turbulent chiefs, and teaching them a lesson too impressive to be forgotten, that the rights of a citizen of the United States shall not be violated with impunity. Hundreds of our people, in the pursuit of their lawful business, are captured yearly, enslaved, and barbarously put to death, without attracting the attention of government, whereas if the hundredth part of the same outrages were committed by any enlightened nation, it would call upon the people to fly to arms. For my own part, I do not see why the arm of authority should not be stretched forth to protect the outraged citizen at the headwaters of the

Guadaloupe with the same promptness it is to protect him in Paraguay, or on the Gulf of Mexico.

The camp of the Spotted Leopard, as has previously been seen, was situated at the source of the Boge Lescoha, at the foot of a mountain range. Fifty miles south, at the other extremity of the valley, were his planting grounds, where a small village had been constructed, and where a number of the tribe, principally squaws, usually remained.

I had been here several months when a party arrived from the plantation, among whom I observed were three white women, notwithstanding their faces were painted. The contour of their features, and especially their red hair, indicated the race to which they belonged, beyond mistake. At the next festival of the full moon, where all bond and free, were permitted to mingle and converse, I found, to my surprise, they could speak English. It was the first time since my capture that I had heard the accents of my native tongue. The oldest woman had passed the age of sixty, and her name was Mrs. Marietta Haskins. The two younger were her daughters, the oldest, Margaret, perhaps, twenty-one, the other, Harriet, three years her junior. They appeared to be persons who had been brought up in humble circumstances, though possessing a fair share of intelligence. The following is, substantially, the version of their story.

They were natives of one of the midland counties of England, where they occupied an obscure, though comfortable position in life. While thus situated, happy and contented with their lot, there came into the vicinity of their residence, one of the Latter-Day Saints, preaching and expounding the Mormon doctrines. His arguments were so ingenious—his appeals so eloquent and earnest—his description of the valley of the Great Salt Lake so glowing that many of the poor people listened and were converted. He represented the climate as more salubrious—the soil more fertile—the scenery more delicious than in any other region of the world. He portrayed, in fascinating colors, the life of ease and luxury the poorest thrall in England might lead in that favored land—where wild herds, the common property of all, darkened a thousand hills, and the bountiful earth yielded its fruits without toil.

The fortunate inhabitants of this paradise he pictured as basking in the full fruition of the highest earthly happiness. Discarding the false, domestic notions to which the wicked and perverse generation around them still clung, they followed the examples of Solomon and the patriarchs of old. They were, he declared, the elect people of God—members of the true church of Jesus Christ of Latter-Day Saints—founded on the revelations contained in the Book of Mormon—delivered unto mankind through the instrumentality of Joseph Smith; and since that great Prophet had suffered death for righteousness' sake, his mantle had descended upon a faithful apostle, Brigham Young, a perfect and upright man.

Seduced into fanaticism, many gathered together their worldly goods, bade adieu to the friends of their youth, and the burial places of their fathers, and departed, with joyful hearts, for that distant region of enchantment. Among those who were led astray by these high-wrought descriptions and fervent appeals was her husband. She, herself, combated the pernicious doctrines, and resisted, as wild and visionary, the idea of quitting home and country for such a far-off place; but the resolution of her husband overcame all opposition, he remaining confident, as if it had been revealed to him from on High, that when they arrived in the valley of the Great Salt Lake and were permitted to enjoy the ministrations of Brigham Young, the successor of the Prophet Joseph, they would enter upon a new and happier existence, to be compared only with that millennial time "when the lion and the lamb shall lie down together, and a little child shall lead them"!

Accordingly, they set out upon the journey, bringing with them their two daughters, leaving behind them one, a married woman, in Devonshire, and after a prosperous voyage, landed at Indianola on Matagorda Bay. The entire party numbered between one and two hundred. Here they made up a wagon train, breaking many cows to the yoke, thinking they would be of service on the way, packed their household goods, furnished themselves with provisions, and started through the Indian country toward the distant city of the Great Salt Lake.

They struck the Rio Grande at Eagle Pass, pushed onward beyond the furthermost settlements, and for a month were slowly winding among the mountains, when many of their teams began to fail. A party of forty were thus compelled to fall in the rear, and finally became separated from their companions. With this party was the Haskins family.

They now began to be annoyed by the Indians. For several days they had been seen scouring the prairies in different directions, ascertaining, perhaps, the strength and quality of the train. They constantly grew bolder and bolder, in the daytime dashing up within a short distance, and at night driving off more and more of their cattle, until, at length, they were destitute of sufficient force to proceed. In this helpless state, they were surrounded by a cloud of savages, and taken prisoners.

In this party of forty were fourteen women and several young infants. The men, among whom, of course, the husband and father, were massacred without exception, the women less fortunate, and the infants were carried away. I turn with disgust from the contemplation of the cruelty to which these captive women were subjected by the lustful hellhounds as they bore them off in triumph to their camps. Some idea of their barbarous nature may be conceived from the fact that while on the way, when an infant cried, it would be snatched from its mother's breast, a hole cut under its chin, then hung on the point of a broken limb, and there left to linger through its little painful life. In this manner, I was assured by Mrs. Haskins and her daughters, every child unable to comprehend the danger of crying was disposed of.

On arriving at a large Indian village, the spoils were divided and distributed among the victors. These women fell into the hands of a chief, who transferred them, a short time after, to the Spotted Leopard. The mother, whose health had broken down under the hardships and sufferings she had endured, was made a common drudge in the camp, while the daughters were appropriated by two burly warriors, and compelled to serve them, both in the capacity of slaves and wives.

When I met with them, they had been with the tribe of the Spotted Leopard between two and three years. In the meantime the mother had grown extremely feeble, and latterly was so afflicted with rheumatism that she was incapable of performing any kind of labor. Of no further service in the camp, there was still enough of life left in her to gratify their thirst for cruelty. Assembling one day outside the town, near the close of my sojourn among them, she was brought forth, stripped, and fastened to the stake. The daughters, likewise, were bound to stakes directly in front of her, so that it was impossible for them to avoid witnessing her agonies.

The same infernal orgies were again gone through with which attended the cruel butchery of Martin and Stewart by the warriors of Big Wolf. Like them, she was first scalped, then cut and hacked with flints, and finally tomahawked, but not until long after life had become extinct. She fainted when the scalp was severed from her head, once or twice revived and screamed, fainting immediately again; and when the final blow was given, it fell upon a corpse! The daughters, likewise, screamed and swooned, and then revived to scream and swoon again; and when the mad rites were ended, were borne back, half-dead, amidst taunts and laughter, to their tents.

These women, and doubtless many others like them, are now dragging out their weary lives in misery and captivity. Humanity pleads in their behalf. Would to God some pitying voice in the councils of the nation would so call attention to their unhappy state that measures would be adopted, as they might be, that would reach them in those lonely wilds, and bring them out of bondage.

CHAPTER 14

The Rolling Thunder was a frequent visitor at our camp, subsequent to the time when he and his tribe accompanied us home from the buffalo hunt. He exhibited a regard for me, and would often fall into a profound revery, when Kianceta, the Weasel, had presented me the watch, and I had caused it to communicate intelligence from the Great Spirit in the usual, rattling offhand manner in which it was accustomed to converse. His interviews with the Spotted Leopard became so long, and, to all appearances, of such vast importance that I had no doubt I was to be subjected to another sale and assignment.

My surmises proved to be entirely correct. Just previous to the time when preparations are made for the annual buffalo hunt, the Spotted Leopard and some of his distinguished warriors, Kianceta, and his other wives, with myself and a considerable drove of pack mules, set off over the mountains in all respect similar to those I had previously crossed, and after a journey of several days, at length entered a large town of, perhaps, two hundred tents, situated in a narrow, but luxuriant valley, over which the thoughtful and sedate Rolling Thunder had the honor to preside. On our arrival, the customary dances were duly performed—the bloody covenant of the square stick was solemnly renewed—the purchase money, consisting of skins and animals, was delivered in due form of savage law—and Kianceta, the Weasel, having braided into my long hair an incredible number of beads, as a parting token of friendship and affection, the Spotted Leopard, followed by his attendants, disappeared from my sight, thank God, forever.

The price paid for me on this occasion, so far as I could judge, exceeded even the price paid on the former sale; my value, in connection with the watch, bearing somewhat the same proportion to that of other, less fortunate captives, as the value of such trotting celebrities as "Ethan Allen," "Flora Temple," and "The Spirit of the Times" does in that of ordinary nags.

A description of one Indian village is, substantially, a description of all others. The same fashion of tents, the same regularity of streets, the same square in the center, characterize them all. The village of Rolling Thunder was situated in a more contracted valley than that of Big Wolf's or the Spotted Leopard's; in other respects it was the same. He had not neglected to take advantage of the privilege apertaining to his patriarchal office; consequently, he, likewise, had gathered into his tents four conjugal companions, whose euphonical names I here mention in the order of their ages. They were So-waw, An-a-wak-he-o, Ho-wawk-ke-no, and Se-ma-naw, the Wise. The latter took charge of the watch, preserving it with all the care and tenderness that had distinguished her illustrious predecessors, Moko and Kianceta, the Weasel.

Se-ma-naw, the youngest wife of the civil chief, possessed a cheerful and lively disposition, always frolicsome as the young antelope of the prairie. She was the daughter of the war chief of the tribe, Sa-was-saw, the Bear, and niece of An-a-wak-ke-o, who was her father's sister. The name of the prophet was Han-na-nos-ka-a, signifying the wisest of the wise.

The Rolling Thunder possessed a remarkably inquisitive mind, and was, moreover, extremely sociable. In the course of his life, he had several times crossed the borders of the Indian territory into Mexico, and had some faint notions of civilization—just enough to excite his curiosity. Hour after hour he would converse with me in his tent about the manners and customs of the whites. On these occasions, I endeavored to illustrate, in the best possible manner, their superiority and power. With a piece of charcoal, I would sketch on a sheet of birch bark the figure of a ship, "with wings whiter than a swan's and wider than many eagles"—its masts taller than the tallest cedar on the mountains—representing it as capable of carrying more than a thousand pack mules could bear; that in this great canoe, the white man would sail away over the salt water, beyond the sight of land, to a vast continent, distant more than a hundred days' journey to the east. He had never seen the ocean; nevertheless, he comprehended its vastness through the traditions of his fathers, who once dwelt upon its shore; but no logic could convince him that the mighty land beyond it was a part of this globe; his reasoning leading him irresistibly to the conclusion that it must necessarily belong to another planet. When I told him the earth was round like a ball, and on the opposite side were extensive countries and millions of people—that if we could bore a hole through it directly beneath our feet, we would emerge into those countries, he laughed me to scorn, arguing that its inhabitants would have to walk with their heads downward, and must necessarily fall off; besides, the premise upon which rested the superstructure of the argument was false, inasmuch as the earth was not round, but flat, a fact patent to the naked eye.

I described a train of cars, wooden tents placed above rolling wheels, filled with a crowd of people outnumbering all his tribe, forced by the power of steam, such as he saw rise from the water boiling in his kettle, along an iron trail, faster than he ever saw the wild horse run across the prairie—endeavored to explain how they could converse, however distant from each other, through the marvelous electric telegraph, describing the immensity of their towns, the number of their warriors; in fine, whether under his own tent in the village, or encamped on the prairie after a day's hunt, he was constantly interrogating me upon some subject connected with their manners, customs, or inventions. Usually, when I had concluded, the old man would remain silent a long time, absorbed in deep study, from which he would, at length, arouse and exclaim— "Wonderful wonderful! are the works of the white man, but the Great Spirit will destroy them all!"

The Rolling Thunder evidently entertained a favorable opinion of me. This was shown soon after my arrival in his camp, by insisting that I should take a wife. I took the matter into serious consideration, endeavoring to decide in my own mind what effect it might have on the chances of escape. The conclusion was that the effect would be favorable, and, accordingly, I signified to the chief that "Barkis was willin'."

The next step was to make a selection from the dusky daughters of the tribe, a matter about which I felt disposed to be somewhat fastidious. The chief sent for some half-dozen, submitting them to my inspection, before a choice was made. Some of them were hideous, either lank and cadaverous, or fat and flabby, having a fiery red new moon painted over each eye, and the full moon in the center of the forehead. These were rejected without hesitation or ceremony. At length one was brought that was pronounced entirely satisfactory. She was small and slender, very young and very agile. There was the grace of nature in her carriage, and, besides, she was not quite as filthy as her companions. She was arrayed in the latest Indian fashion when brought in for examination, wearing prettily embroidered moccasins, colored leggins, calico short gown of many colors, with a great diversity of beads braided profusely in her hair. She was distinguished as the most expert swimmer and deepest diver in the tribe; wherefore, they had bestowed upon her the name of To-ma-no-a-ku-no, the Sleek Otter. Altogether, she was rather a dirty but very comely maiden, in no wise equal to Kianceta, the Weasel, but much fairer than the great majority of her race. With her I entered into the holy estate of matrimony for the space of one moon. After the wedding festivities, the squaws generously assisted her in building a tent, bringing in presents of buffalo skins wherewithal to construct it, after the fashion of a donation party; and when it was finished, we moved in and "went to keeping house." The Sleek Otter made me a faithful and affectionate wife, skinned the deer, cooked the venison, pounded the corn, mended my moccasins, and in all respects performing her conjugal duties with cheerfulness and alacrity. The course of true love ran so smooth that we glided harmoniously through the third moon, and, therefore, became irrevocably joined.

Subsequent to the marriage my privileges were very much enlarged, it being considered improbable, I suppose, that I would tear myself away from the partner of my bosom. I was no longer made the center-post at their war dances, but permitted to wear the gayly colored feathers in my hair, and with the warriors, "round about the cauldron stout, to dance right merrily." But I was by no means entirely at liberty, nor did their apprehensions that I would escape, if opportunity occurred, entirely vanish. I was not allowed to leave the village alone, nor to carry arms. My duties were those of an attendant upon the chief. He kept me near him always, whether on buffalo hunts or visits to the neighboring tribes. He frequently made these visits, when they required but one day's ride, with no one accompanying him but myself. At such times he was mounted on a powerful horse, armed with bow and arrow and a musket—a tomahawk hanging from the pommel of his saddle, and a long knife in his belt; while I rode before him on a sluggish mule, entirely unarmed. "We never passed the night together alone on one of these excursions. In a thousand little ways it was made evident he did not regard it exactly safe to place himself within my power.

The most thrilling incident I witnessed during my sojourn with the tribe of the Rolling Thunder was an Indian duel. Among his warriors were two young men, both proud and spirited, between whom there had long existed a deadly animosity. The cause of their quarrel I could never fully understand, further than it appeared there was a young squaw in the case. Time and time again their differences had been brought before the council without any adjustment being satisfactorily effected. At length, when negotiation had become useless, it was determined to settle the matter forever in a most bloody manner.

It was a pleasant morning towards the close of autumn, when the whole tribe, save the squaws and papooses, assembled on a level piece of ground a mile from the village. Here they formed a large ring, into which walked the Rolling Thunder and Han-na-nos-ka-a, the prophet. The latter pronounced a long discourse, setting forth, as nearly as my imperfect knowledge of the language enabled me to comprehend, the original cause of the quarrel, a detailed account of its progress, the inability of the council to agree upon a satisfactory arrangement, and that, finally, it had been referred to the just decision of the Great Spirit, into whose presence their implacable brethren were now about to appear.

Having concluded, the brothers of the young warriors conducted them into the ring. One of them was, perhaps, twenty-two or twenty-three years of age, the other four or five years older. The younger was somewhat the largest, though both were remarkably athletic and powerful. When they reached the center of the ring, meeting from opposite directions, their left arms, as far up as the elbow, were firmly lashed together with stout, thick cords of buffalo hide. They were bound so thoroughly that the possibility of breaking away from each other was utterly beyond question.

Into the right hand of each was then placed a hunting knife, having a heavy buckhorn handle and a blade about nine inches long, evidently prepared for the occasion by being brought to a keen edge on both sides. The brothers then withdrew some twenty feet from the combatants, drawing from their belts similar knives, when the signal was given and the fight began. After that there was no call of "time"—no retreating to the "corner"—no planting the left heavily on the "mug"—they "toed the scratch" but once, and ended the combat in a single "round."

The battle lasted but a moment, the bright blades, in the meantime, glittering and glimmering in the sun, and the contestants instantly presenting the appearance of men suddenly overtaken by a storm of blood. At length, a mortal thrust by one was followed by a fierce blow from the other, gashing through the side of the neck, from which the purple tide of life spouted up in a high wide arch, when both fell lifeless to the ground.

Had either survived the conflict, according to their code of honor, it would have been the duty of his brother to have put him immediately to death. Throughout the exciting scene not the slightest partiality was exhibited. The faintest shadow of emotion could not be detected upon the countenances of the savage stoics as they gazed upon it. They were stretched side by side on the spot where they had fallen—buried in the customary manner—and left to rest together in peace, at last.

The week succeeding this tragedy, a party of ten or twelve, including the Rolling Thunder and myself, started on a long journey, its object being to ascertain whether the buffalo droves had changed their feeding grounds, before the warriors set out on their annual hunt. In the course of this trip we crossed a valley, the singular appearance of which has very frequently since been the subject of study and reflection.

On the summit of many of the mountains we passed, were broad, level tablelands, destitute of a solitary tree, and covered with rank grass. Upon every one of these elevated plains was to be seen a mound, in most instances in the form of a half-circle, resembling the overgrown ruins of an ancient fortress, and plainly the work of human hands.

Finally we descended into a ravine, walled on either side by rugged cliffs which led us a day's ride to the southwest, when we emerged into a valley about four miles wide and thirty long. It was surrounded on all sides by very high mountains, exceedingly bleak and barren. There was not a tree, or bush, or even a blade of grass to be discovered over the entire surface of the valley. It was covered, to the average depth of fifteen feet, as near as I could judge, with broken pumice stone, a substance precisely similar to the lava of Vesuvius. That it was the result of volcanic eruptions there was no possible doubt, inasmuch as numerous tracts down which it had flowed from the mountaintops were distinctly visible.

The Rolling Thunder, in order to convince me of the correctness of a belief, universal throughout the Comanche nation, conducted me to the western side of this strange valley, where I saw, with infinite astonishment and surprise, the dilapidated ruins of a large town. In the midst of the falling walls of a great number of buildings, which, in some remote age, beyond doubt, had lined spacious streets, was what appeared to have been a church or cathedral. Its walls of cut stone, two feet thick, and in some places fifteen feet high, included a space measuring two hundred feet in length, and, perhaps, one hundred in width. The inner surface of the walls in many places was adorned with elaborate carved work, evidently the labor of a master hand, and at the eastern end was a massive stone platform which seemed to have been used as a stage or pulpit. In my surprise at beholding so unexpectedly these evidences of civilization in that wild region, I turned to the Rolling Thunder and asked if he could explain it.

This is the legend of the Comanches, as he related it: Innumerable moons ago, a race of white men, ten feet high, and far more rich and powerful than any white people now living here inhabited a large range of country, extending from the rising to the setting sun. Their fortifications crowned the summits of the mountains, protecting their populous cities situated in the intervening valleys. They excelled every other nation which has flourished, either before or since, in all manner of cunning handicraft—were brave and warlike—ruling over the land they had wrested from its ancient possessors with a high and haughty hand. Compared with them the palefaces of the present day were pigmies, in both art and arms. They drove the Indians from their homes, putting them to the sword, and occupying the valleys in which their fathers had dwelt before them since the world began. At length, in the height of their power and glory, when they remembered justice and mercy no more and became proud and lifted up, the Great Spirit descended from above, sweeping them with fire and deluge from the face of the earth. The mounds we had seen on the tablelands were the remnants of their fortresses, and the crumbling ruins that surrounded us all that remained of a mighty city.

In like manner, continued the Rolling Thunder, the day will surely come when the present white race, which is driving the Indians before it, and despoiling them of their inheritance, and which, in the confidence of its strength, has become arrogant and boastful and forgotten God, will be swept from existence. For the Great Spirit is just—and as certainly as the rivers flow downward towards the salt sea, or the sun rises in the morning and sets at night, so certainly will He yet restore the land of their fathers to the red man, when the days of his affliction are passed.

It would, indeed, be difficult to adopt any other hypothesis than the one entertained by the chief. The evidence before me was too clear and palpable to be controverted, that at some period, more or less remote, this valley had been inhabited by a people skilled in architecture and evidently possessing, in a high degree, a knowledge of mechanism and the arts. Whether the Rolling Thunder's account of their destruction is correct, or his belief that their successors will eventually be disposed of in the same summary manner is orthodox, will admit of argument; nevertheless, there is no doubt that, in common with all the tribes of the Comanches, he entertains this belief, in genuine sincerity. It is this unwavering faith in the future ascendancy of the red man, and the final restoration to him of all the possessions he has lost, which prompts him to perpetual resistance, and which so often led the Rolling Thunder to exclaim, after I had described some marvelous invention—"Wonderful, wonderful are the works of the white man, but the Great Spirit will destroy them all."

After leaving the volcanic valley and ascertaining the feeding grounds of the bison, we returned to the village, and soon again set forth on the yearly buffalo hunt. It is a singular fact that on these excursions the hunters are followed by droves of wolves. They seem to have an instinctive knowledge of the business in which the party is about to engage. As soon as the skin is stripped from the buffalo they surround the carcass and devour it. To wake in the dead of night, after dreaming, peradventure, of early home and friends, to find yourself under a rude tent, in those far distant wilds, surrounded by a savage tribe, produces sensations, lonely and desolate indeed—but terror mingles with the sense of desolation when, all around, the adjacent solitudes are vocal with the barking and snarling and howling of wolves, gorging themselves at their midnight feasts.

It was at such times as these my soul longed to reach once more the abodes of civilized man. Though greatly discouraged, I never entirely despaired of sooner or later effecting an escape. Aside from the charm which still lingered around the watch, the silver child of the sun, that had so providentially shielded me from unspeakable outrage during the earlier portion of my captivity, I was confident the covenant of blood into which I had entered, and more than all, my marriage with Sleek Otter, would henceforth save me from violence.

At this time I had no apprehensions whatever in regard to my personal safety so long as I remained an obedient captive, fulfilling the humble duties imposed upon me. A detected attempt at escape, however, I was fully aware, would be followed by the severest penalties. I had so long, and so intensely, contemplated the subject that there was no possible aspect in which it could present itself that had not received the closest and most careful scrutiny and consideration. Of one thing I had become thoroughly convinced, which was that if I had been successful in escaping from the tribe of the Spotted Leopard, without the means of killing game or making a fire, I should, most assuredly, have perished from starvation among the mountains.

It became necessary, therefore, to devise some plan by which, in case the opportunity offered, I could provide myself with these indispensable conveniences. It is probable I could, on many occasions, have reached the mountains unperceived after the marriage, had the attempt been made, but it was utterly impossible to have done so, providing myself at the same time with any kind of arms—the watchfulness over me in respect to them being strict and constant.

It was while indulging in these never-ending speculations that the Rolling Thunder ordered me to saddle my mule and accompany him on a long journey. It should be remembered by the reader that I have now brought down this narrative to the month of May last, wherefore the object of the journey upon which the Indian chief, at this point, is ready to depart, and which I gathered, both from himself and various other sources, may be regarded in many quarters as exceedingly important.

His destination was a village three days' journey to the north. At this place a general convention had been called, to be composed of all the chiefs of all the different tribes inhabitating the country between the northern bounds of Mexico and the regions of perpetual snow. The object of the convention was to induce the Indian nations, hitherto at variance, to bury the hatchet as between themselves, smoke the peace pipe, and unite in a universal bond of brotherhood, for the purpose of preventing the whites from passing through their territories to the settlements on the Pacific Coast.

It was, as I then understood it, and now believe, to enter into an alliance with the view of waging an exterminating and implacable war upon every train of emigrants or other party moving towards California, Oregon, the Great Salt Lake, or other points in either of those directions. How it terminated, circumstances unanticipated but of a most exciting and stirring character forbid my knowing, yet, that the design was precisely such as I have mentioned is a fact, which I beg all those who contemplate making the overland route to bear seriously in mind.

The Rolling Thunder, before taking his departure, arrayed himself with extraordinary care. A dozen scalps were attached to his war shirt; silver trinkets representing the moon in all its phases were fastened on his breast; his feet were clad in new and cunningly embroidered moccasins, and on his head rested a crown of feathers plucked from the crow, the kingfisher, the prairie hen, and the eagle, so dyed by his ingenious wives as to reflect all the colors of the rainbow. Of all the horses that grazed the wide pastures round about his camp, he was mounted upon the most fleet and spirited— the weapons of war in which he was accoutred were a knife thrust through his belt, a hatchet suspended from the pommel of his saddle, and a

Mexican rifle, rare among his tribe, upon the possession of which he prided himself exceedingly.

I bestrode the same old mule that had so often and so far borne me on her back, with nothing hanging from my saddlebow but a huge buffalo horn wherewith to furnish my doughty master with cool draughts from the streams as we journeyed on the way. Saluting the Sleek Otter, who little thought it was the last nod she would ever receive from her long-haired spouse—for, not having seen a razor for three years, I was very far from being "the man all shaven and shorn, who married the maiden all forlorn"—we trotted away from the village, myself in advance, neither of us destined ever to return.

From early morning we traveled leisurely but steadily, and at sunset entered a valley wherein resided a small tribe whose chief was Nis-ti-u-na, the Wild Horse. The usual hospitalities were extended—or rather on this occasion they were unusual—inasmuch as a party had just returned from a meeting with the traders, bringing with them a quantity of mescal, a kind of whisky distilled from the fruit of a tree, commonly known in Mexico as the cabbage tree.

An Indian's dignity, whether chief or subject, never rises to that elevated degree which prevents his getting drunk every opportunity that offers, and consequently it followed, as a matter of course, that so distinguished a visitor as the Rolling Thunder, arrived at that peculiar juncture, could not avoid stretching himself on his buffalo skin that night without a weighty "brick in his hat." In other words, the sedate old fellow became beastly intoxicated—forgot altogether the decorum that characterized his customary walk and conversation—vainly attempted to be funny—danced out of place—and whooped when there was no occasion for it— in fact, was as boisterous and silly as about half a gallon of bad whiskey could make him.

However, bright and early in the morning, the chief was again on his proper legs, ready to set forward on the journey, intending to lodge that night at another village farther to the north. After a breakfast of mustang steak, which rested ill on his sour stomach, we bade the sore-headed sons of the tribe of the Wild Horse good morning, and pursued our travel. Very soon we passed out of their valley and entered the defiles of the mountains. The last night's debauch had set the old chief on fire, and before the sun had halfway ascended to the zenith, his throat was parched, and he was mad with thirst. But there was no water to be found. On and on we went, threading our way through thick bushes, around the sharp points of overhanging cliffs, across rough and rugged ravines, but nowhere did a spring or running stream greet his longing eyes. We continued to press forward in this manner until about one o'clock in the afternoon, when, reaching the bottom of a deep hollow, we discovered water oozing from the base of a perpendicular precipice and trickling down a little muddy channel through the grass.

He called impetuously upon me to fill the horn at once. Though I attempted to obey his order with all possible celerity, the rill was so extremely shallow that in spite of my best endeavors, every dip I made, the contents of the horn would come up in the proportion of three parts mud to one of water. Perceiving the difficulty, he leaped from his horse, directing me to hold him by the bridle, threw his Mexican rifle on the ground, and laying down upon it in the grass, thrust his scorched lips into the little stream.

Standing by the horse's side, I observed the hatchet hanging from the pommel of the saddle. The thought flashed through my mind quick as the fierce lightning that the hour of my deliverance had come at last, and snatching it, in that instant, from its place, I leaped towards him, burying the dull edge a broad hand's breadth in his brain. A moment sufficed to draw the rifle from beneath him, jerk the long knife from his girdle, mount his horse, and dash wildly away over an unknown path, towards the land of freedom.

CHAPTER 15

Turning about, I retraced the path we had followed, some two miles, remembering to have seen a narrow defile stretching to the west as we passed along. Plunging into this, I spurred on at a breakneck pace, over piles of broken stones that had rolled down from the declivities, penetrated barricades of tangled thorns and brushwood, the mule all the while following closely at the horse's heels, and at the end of six miles, encountered a bold bluff extending entirely across the western termination of the ravine, abruptly arresting any further progress in that direction.

This bluff was the eastern side of a high, bleak, rocky spur, which shot out from a still more elevated range, right athwart the path I was pursuing. Wheeling northward and moving along its base, I reached, at length, a contracted crevice, half-filled with broken, sharp-angled fragments of rock, up which, with great difficulty, myself, horse, and mule managed to clamber, until we gained a comparatively level spot, a kind of terrace, some twenty feet wide, about halfway to the summit. Further ascent was impossible, and no other recourse was left but to follow the terrace whithersoever it led. Its surface presented, as an Indian would term it, a clear trail, and was undoubtedly one of the paths traversed by deer and other animals while migrating from one feeding ground to another. We followed it as it wound around the southern declivity of the precipice, becoming more and more narrow as we advanced, until, to my unutterable horror, it had contracted to a width less than two feet. A sharp point round which it circled just in front of me hid the view beyond, but all appearances indicated it terminated there. On one side were great, loose overhanging rocks impossible to ascend and threatening to fall, on the other, an almost perpendicular descent of at least a hundred feet. The horse hesitated to proceed, as if conscious of the danger to which he was exposed. Between the wall of adamant on the right and the precipice on the left, there was not sufficient room to enable either horse or mule to turn around, and so entirely did their bodies fill up the path it was impracticable for me to turn back, had it become necessary so to do, without pushing the poor brutes down the fearful steep.

With eyes turned away from the dizzy depth below, down which, in my despair, a strange impulse urged me to plunge and end a miserable life at once, I crawled carefully to the sharp point before me, closely hugging the upper side, and peering round it, beheld with ineffable satisfaction that it expanded into a broad, smooth road. Much urging and coaxing, finally succeeded in inducing the horse to pass the point of danger. My sense of relief, when we had reached a place of safety, was like that of the awakened sleeper when he thanks God the awful chasm over which he has been hanging by a slender twig is but the vagary of a dream.

From the spot now gained, I gazed abroad upon the surrounding scene, and a wilder or more dreary one never broke upon my vision. On all sides around and above, were piled mountain upon mountain as far as the eye could reach. Here and there, among the defiles, could be discovered strips of timber, but the summits, as they appeared in the distance, were bare and rocky, their bald peaks stretching to the clouds.

After some examination, for I was in too great haste to linger, a narrow opening in a southwest direction attracted my attention, and towards it I turned my steps. The descent, though not entirely impracticable, was tedious in the extreme. The ledges were numerous and abrupt, and difficult to pass, often drawing me far out of a straight course. Finally, however, the opening was reached, proving to be another ravine averaging two hundred yards in width, over which were scattered cedar trees and clusters of thick bushes. By the time I had reached the southwestern termination of this little solitary valley, the sun had set, and darkness was fast spreading over the earth. Pushing into the center of a dense thicket, covering perhaps two or three acres, the loneliest spot that presented itself, I halted for the night.

Securing the horse to a limb by the bridle, and removing the buffalo-skin saddle, I sat down upon it and consulted with myself as to what it was best to do. My safety depended much upon circumstances. If the body of the chief should happen to be discovered immediately, my escape was doubtful. The moment it was found, my knowledge of savage life taught me, a party would instantly and eagerly start upon my trail, and at the same time messengers be sent to all the tribes far and near, calling on them to keep a sharp lookout for my approach, so that I had as much to apprehend in front as in the rear.

I was provided with the dead chief's rifle and ammunition, and consequently had the means of kindling a fire, but making the one or discharging the other, at least for some days, would be a dangerous experiment, inasmuch as the noise of the rifle or the light of the fire might expose me. The demands of appetite, however, would render it necessary to risk both, and, in fact, already were they becoming clamorous, having fasted since our early departure in the morning from the camp of the Wild Horse. Being impossible at that hour to capture game, my thoughts turned upon the mule. She had followed me unexpectedly and could be of no possible use; on the contrary, in all probability, would prove an annoyance. Necessity, which is, indeed, the mother of invention, suggested how I could turn her to account, and the suggestion was adopted. Walking up to the tired and patient beast, as unsuspicious of harm as was her now stark owner when he bent down to drink, I grasped the long knife that was wont to grace his girdle, and drew it across her throat.

When life was extinct, I cut from her hams long thin slips of flesh to the measure of some ten pounds, and having done so, resolved to run the venture of kindling a fire, trusting that the Rolling Thunder was still reposing undiscovered and undisturbed where I had left him. Accordingly, I gathered a pile of sticks, and withdrawing the charge from the rifle, ignited a priming of powder which presently resulted in a ruddy, and under other circumstances, a cheerful blaze. The mule meat was then broiled, and satisfying present appetite upon a portion, the remainder was carefully laid aside for future necessity. Thus provided with provisions for several days to come, it occurred to me that I might suffer for the lack of water on those thirsty mountains. The buffalo horn, though convenient at a stream or spring, could not be used in carrying away their contents. Some kind of vessel was indispensable, and in order to be furnished with such an article, I cut the bladder from the mule, blew it up, dried it by the fire, filled it from a sluggish pool at hand, tying the mouth with a strong buffalo string.

These labors performed, with the reloaded rifle in my hands, I sat down on the buffalo skin at the foot of a cedar tree and leaned against its trunk. Here, a new terror awaited me I had not anticipated. The mule's blood had been scented by wild beasts, wolves and panthers, which began to scream. Nearer and nearer they approached until the horse snuffed and snorted, and I could hear their teeth snap, and the dry sticks crackle beneath their feet. A dozen times I was on the point of ascending the tree, momentarily expecting to be attacked. With such a crash would they break through the thicket that many times I bounded to my feet, thinking the Indians were upon me. It was a fearful night, and the most fearful sound that has ever fallen on my ears is the scream of the panther, so like is it to the plaintive, agonizing shriek of a human being. The fortunate resolution I had taken to build a fire undoubtedly kept them off, and the absence of Indians beyond the sound of their unearthly confusion was the sole cause of my hiding place not being disclosed. It taught me, however, a lesson not thenceforward to be forgotten, that is to say, never to encamp where I had killed my game.

In the morning, very early, I proceeded on the journey, and in the course of half an hour was again intercepted by another mountain. It was high noon, when I reached the summit, so rough and difficult was the ascent. Often, having entered a gully whose entrance allured me with the promise of a favorable path, I would break through dense thickets of prickly pear, the thorns piercing and tearing my flesh, until thinking I was about to emerge upon the plateau above, a wall of fallen stone, or the trunk of a prostrate tree, would suddenly present an invincible barrier, compelling me to return down the same painful path and seek, in another place, some more feasible passage.

During the afternoon, I kept my course, as near as possible, along the ridge of the highlands, but notwithstanding I improved every moment of the time, so rugged was the route it is probable I had not passed ten miles in a direct line from the place of departure in the morning when night again overtook me. This was passed under a ledge, in a little nook where a portion of the rock, in the form of a wedge, had fallen out. On such an eminence as this it would have been madness to light a fire—nothing less than a signal to any in pursuit to come up and take me—nevertheless, the tough mule meat, and the yet unemptied bladder, furnished me with a thankful repast. My poor horse, however, was not so well supplied, there being neither water or grass here, and but few bushes on which to browse. Wrapping the buffalo skin around me, I endeavored to sleep, realizing the invigoration it would bring was necessary to sustain the fatigue and hardship before me; but my slumbers were broken and troubled, full of fearful dreams, in which I was clamboring over rocks or pursued by Indians, yelling close on my trail, and yet, unable to fly, having lost the power to move, so that I arose with the first faint glimpse of the rising sun, sore and unrefreshed.

I continued along the height a portion of this day, and would have pursued it further, deeming it safer than a less elevated path, had it not become absolutely necessary to find water for my horse. This necessity induced me to make my way down the mountain side, a labor I succeeded in achieving towards the close of the day, when I struck a green, delicious valley, a mile wide in some parts, on which wild horses, a few buffalo, deer, and antelope were grazing, and which apparently stretched a long distance to the south. Fearing to adventure upon it in daylight, I hid in a cedar copse until dark, when, allowing the horse to slake his thirst at a rivulet, and feed an hour on the rank grass, I mounted and rode as fast as I could urge him until long after midnight, keeping in the shadows of the mountains. I had ridden in this manner at least thirty miles, congratulating myself on the rapid progress I was making, when the little valley came to a point, shut in by impassable precipices.

The opening day disclosed that I had been completely entrapped. The valley was surrounded on all sides by precipitous rocks, up which, in some places, I might possibly have made my way alone, but which it was beyond the power of the horse to ascend. My situation now became unpleasant, it being probable that a luxuriant valley like this, abounding in game and so rarely to be found amidst these sterile regions, must be frequented by Indians.

No alternative presented itself, but to turn back, retrace, cautiously, the course over which I had galloped with so much satisfaction the previous night. The whole of this day was occupied in traveling about fifteen miles. Along the south side of the valley which I was now coursing, at the average distance from each other of three-fourths of a mile perhaps, narrow points or promontories shot out from the side of the mountains, the space of prairie land lying between them resembling a half-moon or segment of a circle. From the extremity of one of these headlands I would reconnoiter, until satisfied the "coast was clear," then dash across to the next as fast as the horse could run. In this manner, as before stated, some fifteen miles were accomplished which brought me to the close of the day, and also to a path that opened a comparatively easy passage up the steep.

For two days I wandered over these mountains, rising constantly from ridge to ridge until the summit was attained and passed, and at evening of the sixth day of the flight descended into a dark, cavernous defile, where I found a spring of water and many deer browsing around it. The mule meat, besides being so tough as to demand the exercise of my utmost powers of mastication, was now nearly gone. Here, for the first time, I discharged the rifle, bringing down a plump doe, whose skin and hindquarters I carried forward four or five miles and halted for the night, leaving the remainder as an entertainment for the wolves. Selecting a secluded spot under an overhanging cliff, and approached through a thick growth of brushwood, I kindled, for the second time, a fire, and prepared a meal of venison. Though unsalted and unpeppered, and without the concomitants of currant jelly or other desert, after the hard fare upon which I had so long existed, no epicure ever enjoyed with a keener relish the daintiest dish that I did, slice after slice, of the juicy and tender steaks. Venison will remain in a state of preservation longer than the flesh of any animal with which I am acquainted. Notwithstanding the weather was warm, I was not obliged after this to shoot a deer oftener than once in three days.

The seventh day found me toiling over a succession of mountains smoother, and of a more gradual ascent, than any I had yet crossed. My course here led in a southwest direction, having conceived the idea, which subsequently proved very erroneous, that it would conduct me to the Mexican state of Chihuahua. At length, arriving at the height of land, a wide prairie unexpectedly spread out before me, over which numerous Indian horsemen were riding, and at my feet stood an Indian town of at least three hundred tents.

The prairie extended to the west farther than I could perceive, but the mountains that bound its eastern terminus were distinguishable at a distance, as near as I could estimate, of twenty miles. Anxious to escape, at once, from so dangerous a vicinity, I lost no time in coming to a resolution, which was to make the detour of its eastern extremity. In order to do so, however, it was necessary again to retrace my steps many rough and weary miles; but perseverance, incited by an apprehension of immediate danger, enabled me to "overcome all things," insomuch that late in the evening of the day following the discovery of the town I had rounded the point of the prairie and was encamped in a snug and solitary fastness of the mountains that lined its western side. Until I had passed far beyond this Indian settlement, I exercised the same caution as if assured intelligence had been conveyed to them of the death of Rolling Thunder, and as if I knew they were on the watch for my approach.

For nearly two weeks now I was lost in a vast range of mountains, sometimes going forward, at others compelled to turn back, winding through deep hollows, and climbing over abrupt precipices, often suffering with hunger and parched with thirst. I doubt if civilized or savage man ever before or since made the passage of this sterile region. During the day I directed by course by the sun, always keeping in view, as far as practicable, in my zig-zag progress some prominent peak far in the distance. At night I was guided by the North Star. However, there were many cloudy days and nights, during which I was unable to proceed with certainty, and consequently lost much time.

There were many difficulties, hardships, and dangers encountered on this lonesome journey, a correct description whereof it is impossible for me to draw, or the reader to conceive. For instance, I was frightfully annoyed by snakes. It has been seen on a former page that the sight of these reptiles always inspired me with emotions of dread and terror. There was a flat-headed adder I frequently discovered on wet ground and near were everywhere; but there was another species, a kind I had never seen, and am ignorant of the name naturalists have applied to it. It was of a brown color, rather slim, and as often exceeding as falling short of nine feet in length. It inhabited the clefts of the rocks, and stretched itself out on the ledges in the sun. One of its peculiar characteristics was to blow, when disturbed, emitting a loud, disagreeable, unnatural noise, half hiss, half bellow. Frequently while laboring up the steep side of a mountain, drawing myself up a declivity by grasping slight rooted twigs that had sprung up in the cracks and crevices of the rocks, as my head emerged above the surface I was striving to attain, one of these monsters would raise itself to the height of three feet and blow directly in my face. It made my "locks," which, indeed, were "knotted and combined, to part, and each particular hair to stand on end." Bears were numerous, and occasionally a panther could be seen stealing noiselessly through the underwood, but these caused me very little, in fact, no apprehension whatever.

On the twentieth day Indians were again discovered. I had reached another valley early in the morning, and from a secure point was making observations, when I perceived them, to the number of a hundred horsemen, followed by a train of pack mules moving towards the west. There was no village to be seen, and I concluded, therefore, they were a party on a visit to some neighboring tribe, the buffalo-hunting season having passed. Watching them until the last one had disappeared and making myself certain others were not approaching, I hurried over the narrow valley at a rapid pace, and commenced another "crossing of the Alps."

By this time the horse had suffered so much from thirst and the want of forage that he had become emaciated in the extreme. His hoofs, likewise, were broken, and he was lame and spiritless. My moccasins, also, were worn out, my feet covered with bruises, and my whole body sore and stiff.

In this condition we reached, one day, a singular spot, a deep basin among the hills, enclosing bottom land to the extent of ten or fifteen acres, covered alternately with patches of grass and thickets of brush and wholly shut in by lofty eminences. A spring, clear as crystal, gushed from the base of the mountain on one side, and a number of deer were feeding at different points. At this green spot in the desert I remained twelve days.

Though I had no mirror with me to make a particular examination, I expect my personal appearance was not especially attractive. Three years had elapsed since my beard or the hair of my head had defiled a comb, brush, or razor. My moccasins were dilapidated beyond redemption, my leggins and hunting shirt in shreds, torn in a thousand places by thorns and brambles. I still retained the deerskin band which bound my head and fastened on the forehead with a clasp, preventing the hair from falling over my eyes, but the little painted feathers with which the Sleek Otter had ambitiously adorned it, were long since blown to the winds of heaven.

My employments during the twelve days I halted in this solitary place were various. The most laborious portion of each day was spent in ascending one or the other of the adjacent peaks, and taking an observation of the surrounding region, in order to ascertain if an enemy was approaching. With much difficulty I cleared a small space in the center of the densest thicket, cutting out and pulling up the roots, whereon I erected a fireplace of stone, the object of taking so much pains being to kindle the fire where the thick shrubbery about it would, in a great measure, conceal the light. Here I went assiduously at work to provide for "a rainy day," in the matter of provisions, and to replenish my wardrobe. I shot four or five deer at different times, drying as much of the flesh as I deemed it convenient to carry, and manufacturing the skins into necessary articles of wearing apparel. The only tool I possessed was a knife, but with this managed to accomplish all I undertook. The moccasins were made of the hide while in its green state, applied to the foot with the hair inside, fastened with stout whangs of the same material inserted through holes made with the point of the knife and tied, and left in that condition to dry. I was familiar with the Indian mode of dressing buckskin with the brains of the deer itself, and had no difficulty in preparing new leggins and hunting coat. Perhaps the fit was not exactly admirable, nor the suit, taken as a whole, such as would be commended by a fashionable man at a select party; nevertheless, it suited the society with which I was then associating, and was extremely comfortable. I delayed several days after these arrangements were effected on account of the horse, which, notwithstanding he had plenty of pasture and water, did not seem to recruit, but, on the contrary, to be effectually broken down.

However, I set out again at the end of twelve days, arrayed in my "new clothes," and with the bundle of dried venison hanging at the saddle bow, wildly imagining myself in the neighborhood of Santa Fe. My course now led over a mountainous region, if possible more difficult, barren, and desolate than any that had preceded it. Water was rarely to be found, and in many parts there was not sufficient grass on a thousand acres to supply the horse with one night's provender. He constantly became more and more tender-footed and lame, the flesh had departed from his bones, and the proud and fiery spirit with which he had pranced out of his native valley, amidst the salutations of the tribe, with the Rolling Thunder on his back, was gone—completely gone. I was now compelled to lead him, stopping frequently for him to lie down. At length, the supply of water I had brought with me from the last spring was exhausted, and I was obliged to leave him on the mountains.

Rolling up the buffalo skin enclosing my drinking horn and other articles, and tying it with the bridle reins into the form of a knapsack, I threw it upon my back, shouldered the rifle, and bidding the poor horse a sorrowful farewell, started on alone.

Now for the first time my heart died within me. For aught I could discover, the abodes of civilized men were as far off as when I began the long and tedious journey. I began to doubt myself, to fear that I had become crazed and lost, and instead of pursuing the southwesterly course I imagined, was only wandering round and round over the same ever lasting solitudes. Moreover, since parting from the horse, who had been as a companion to me, whose presence during the silent hours of the night, stamping and feeding round me, seemed like a protection, I was lonesome and desolate indeed. And I was sick in body as well as soul. My limbs had become swollen and the wounds and bruises that covered me inflamed and painful.

In this condition of body and mind, several days after my leaving the horse, I came upon a fountain of pure water, gushing out beautifully from a rock. The cool draught was so refreshing and its application to my burning body afforded so much relief, I fully resolved to proceed no further, but there linger through the remainder of my life, which seemed fast waning to its close. A night's rest, however, relieved me somewhat of pain, inspired me with renewed hopes, and animated me to make another attempt to drag myself wearily along. But day by day I grew weaker as I advanced, the vigorous strength and hardy constitution with which Providence had blessed me breaking down under these incessant struggles and privations. Very often while reclining on the ground, my feet resting on some little elevation to relieve pain, it seemed certain that sufficient energy would not return to permit me to rise again, and still more often I prayed God that when I fell asleep I might never wake again.

The fifty-sixth day of my distressing travels brought me to a rolling prairie of considerable extent, dotted with many small groves of timber. Into one of these I had made my way to avoid the hot beams of the sun, and was lying in the shade, in a drowsy, half sleeping state, when I was startled by the sharp crack of a rifle close at hand. My first thought was—is it possible they have chased me so far? Bounding to my feet, I held the rifle in my hands, ready to bring it to an aim as soon as necessity required, resolving, weak as I was, after such incredible suffering to stand on the defense. In the course of some ten minutes, instead of being rushed upon by a band of Indians, a mounted Mexican, wearing a wide-brimmed sombrero, came riding leisurely along, with a deer which had received its death wound from the discharge that had so astounded me, thrown over his horse's back, behind the saddle.

"How do you do?" he exclaimed, in mongrel Spanish, and much astonished.

Not knowing the character of the company into which I had so unexpectedly fallen, and deeming it prudent for safety to conceal my true story for the present, I walked up to him and addressing him in his own language, with which I am familiar, replied, "Sick and dying, will you help me, my friend?"

"How come you here?" he inquired.

"I have been lost among the mountains," I answered, "and have been trying to make my way to the settlements."

Much other conversation ensued, when he informed me he was one of a party of three who had been on a trading expedition to the Apaches, and were now on their return—that his companions were encamped not far distant—that they belonged to San Fernandez, below Eagle Pass, near the Rio Grande, and concluded by inviting me to accompany him to the camp. Perceiving how difficult it was for me to proceed, he dismounted and helped me into the saddle and walked by the side of the horse, conversing kindly, and evidently much interested in my behalf.

His companions were cooking when we arrived, and like himself, were greatly astonished at beholding me. However, they gave me a hospitable and generous welcome, exhibiting the true spirit of the Good Samaritan. In their train were eight pack mules, loaded with buffalo robes and furs, the proceeds of their traffic with the tribes. Their kindness won my entire confidence at once, and without further hesitation I related the whole story of my adventures. The interest my previous story of being lost among the mountains had excited was vastly enhanced by this disclosure, and no pains were now spared to administer to my comfort and convenience. The eight packs were rearranged so as to afford me one of the mules to ride, and we started on.

The third day we crossed the Rio Grande upon a raft, swimming the mules and horses, and passing through a number of frontier settlements, at all of which my misfortunes were related by the traders, and followed by the kindest treatment. On the seventh day thereafter, we entered the town of San Fernandez. The names of these humane and generous men are Antonio Halleno, Josef de Silva and Mario Francisco des Lezzez. I owe them a lasting debt of gratitude which I can only repay by proclaiming their noble-hearted generosity to a poor suffering wanderer among the mountains, wherever this narrative may go.

I remained six weeks at San Fernandez under the care of a physician, at the end of which time Josef de Silva accompanied me to Matamoros. From thence I proceeded to Brazos Santiago and shipped for Havana, where, having fulfilled my parting promise to Aikens to communicate the intelligence of his fate, in case I escaped, to his friend at Corpus Christi, I set sail in the schooner Elizabeth Jones, Captain William Hudson, and on the tenth day of November, 1858, reached the United States.

I cannot conclude this history of my adventures and misfortunes without once more endeavoring to direct attention towards those captives, less fortunate than myself, who still remain among the Indians. My own observation, together with the knowledge obtained from the chiefs and warriors of the tribes to which I was so long attached, places the matter beyond dispute, that a large number of white prisoners, principally women, are held by them.

Their situation, above all others, is eminently one deserving the consideration of humane and philanthropic persons. The barbarity and degradation to which they are doomed, render them, truly, especial objects of pity and compassion, and whoever engages to accomplish their deliverance will enter on a work of Christian charity.

If the proper effort were made in the right direction, beyond question, many of them could be rescued. It would not require an armed invasion of the Indian territory; such an invasion, however salutary it might prove in other respects, would in all probability result disastrously to the captive. There is a peaceful and far more economical mode by which their liberation can be effected, and this is through the instrumentality of the traders.

These compose a privileged class among the savages; are protected rather than injured by them. They are relied upon for their annual supply of knives, hatchets, calico, and trinkets. Arrangements could therefore be made with the traders to purchase the white men and women belonging to the several tribes with which they have intercourse—purchases easily to be negotiated if supplied with the necessary means. In most instances they are without friends, the survivors of emigrant families, attacked and overcome while journeying to the distant West. Bearing always in remembrance the awful scenes of agony and torture it has been my lot to witness, I can never cease to plead with my countrymen to interest themselves in behalf of those who are still in bonds, and subject to the same cruelties; ready, myself, though prematurely old, to devote the remainder of my days, without reward, to the accomplishment of their ransom.

Printed in Great Britain
by Amazon